James Laver

COSTUME AND FASHION
A CONCISE HISTORY

Fifth edition
Penultimate chapter by Amy de la Haye and Andrew Tucker
Concluding chapter by Amy de la Haye

348 illustrations, 85 in colour

 Thames & Hudson world of art

TO MRS DORIS LANGLEY MOORE
COLLECTOR, AUTHOR AND FRIEND

First published in the United Kingdom in 1969 by
Thames & Hudson Ltd, 181A High Holborn, London WC1V 7QX

www.thamesandhudson.com

Chapters 1–9 copyright © 1969 and 1982 James Laver
Chapters 10–11 copyright © 1995, 2002 and 2012
Thames & Hudson Ltd, London

Fifth edition 2012

British Library Cataloguing-in-Publication Data
A catalogue record for this book is available from the British Library

ISBN 978-0-500-20412-2

Printed and bound in Singapore by C.S. Graphics

Contents

1 Venus of Lespugue.
Aurignacian period, France.
Distorted female fertility
figure showing loin-cloth
formed of twisted strands of
wool or flax

CHAPTER ONE

How it all began

COSTUME, throughout the greater part of its history, has followed two separate lines of development, resulting in two contrasting types of garment. The most obvious line of division in modern eyes is between male and female dress: trousers and skirts. But it is by no means true that men have always worn bifurcated clothes and women not. The Greeks and Romans wore tunics, that is to say, skirts. Mountain people like the Scots and the modern Greeks wear what are, in effect, skirts. Far Eastern and Near Eastern women have worn trousers, and many continue to do so. The sex division turns out not to be a true division at all.

It is possible to contrast 'fitted' and 'draped' clothes, most modern clothes falling into the first category and Ancient Greek clothes, for example, into the other. History has shown many variations in this respect, and it is possible to find intermediate types. Perhaps the most useful distinction is that drawn by the anthropologists between 'tropical' and 'arctic' dress.

The great ancient civilizations arose in the fertile valleys of the Euphrates, the Nile and the Indus: all tropical areas, where protection from the cold cannot have been the dominant motive for wearing clothes. Many such motives have been adduced, ranging from the naïve idea, based on the story in Genesis, that clothes were worn for reasons of modesty, to the sophisticated notion that they were worn for reasons of display and protective magic. The psychology of clothes, however, has been adequately dealt with elsewhere. In the present study it is proposed largely to ignore these complications and to concentrate on the two questions of form and material.

2, 3 A seated woman and a king from Mari. Sumerian, c. 2900–2685 BC. Skirt and shawl are built up of twisted tufts of wool or flax arranged in flounces

The early civilizations of Egypt and Mesopotamia are far from being the whole story. Within recent years a much more primitive documentation has become available, largely owing to the discovery and study of cave paintings. Geologists have made us aware of a succession of Ice Ages when the climate of a large part of Europe was extremely cold. Even in the last of the Palaeolithic cultures (that is, cultures in which tools and weapons were made by chipping hard stones like flints) life was lived, as it were, on the edge of the great glaciers which covered much of the continent. In such circumstances, although details of clothing may have been determined by social and psychological considerations, the main motive in covering the body was to keep out the cold, since nature had proved so niggardly in providing *homo sapiens* with a natural coat of fur.

The animals were more fortunate, and primitive man soon realized that they could be hunted and killed not only for their

8

4 The god Abu(?) and a female statue from Tell Asmar. Sumerian, early third millennium B C. The loin-cloth has become recognizably a skirt and the twisted tufts have shrunk to a fringe

flesh but for their pelts. In other words he began to wear furs. This presented him with two problems. Not only was the skin of a beast merely wrapped round the shoulders very hampering to his movements, but it left part of the body exposed. He therefore desired to *shape* it in some way, even if at first he had no means of doing so.

The second problem is that the skins of animals, as they dry, become very hard and intractable. Some method had to be found of making them soft and pliable; the simplest method of doing this is by a laborious mastication. Eskimo women to the present day spend a considerable part of their time *chewing* the hides which their husbands bring home from the chase. Another method consists of alternately wetting the hide and beating it with a mallet, having first scraped off any fragments of flesh which may still be adhering to it. Neither process is very satisfactory, however, for, if the hides become wet, the whole labour has to be repeated.

An advance was made when it was discovered that oil or blubber rubbed into the skin helped to keep it pliable for a longer time, that is, until the oil dried out. The next step was the discovery of tanning, and it is strange to think that the essential techniques of this process, so primitive in their inception, are still in use today. The bark of certain trees, notably the oak and the willow, contains tannic acid which can be extracted by soaking the bark in water. The hides are then immersed for considerable periods in the solution and emerge from this process permanently pliable and waterproof.

Such prepared pelts could also be cut and shaped, and we now come to one of the greatest technological advances in human history, comparable in importance to the invention of the wheel and the discovery of fire: the invention of the eyed needle. Large numbers of such needles, made of mammoth ivory, the bones of the reindeer and the tusks of the walrus, have been found in Palaeolithic caves, where they were deposited forty thousand years ago. Some of them are quite small and of exquisite workmanship. This invention made it possible to sew pieces of hide together to make them fit the body. The result was the kind of clothing still worn by the Eskimo.

Meanwhile, people living in somewhat more temperate climates were discovering the use of animal and vegetable fibres. It is probable that felting was the first step. In this process, developed in Central Asia by the ancestors of the Mongols, wool or hair is combed out, wetted and placed in layers on a mat. The mat is then rolled up tightly and beaten with a stick. The strands of hair or wool are thus matted together and the felt produced is warm, pliable and durable and can be cut and sewn to make garments, rugs and tents.

Another primitive method, also using vegetable fibres, was to make use of the bark of certain trees such as the mulberry or fig. The bark was stripped off and soaked in water. Three layers were then placed on a flat stone, the grain of the middle layer being at right angles to the other two. The layers were then beaten with a mallet until they clung together and the bark cloth resulting was oiled or painted to add to its durability. This process, very similar to that used by the Ancient Egyptians to convert papyrus into a writing material, might be regarded as a half-way house between matting and weaving. Bark cloth, however, is not easily cut or sewn, and garments made of it are usually draperies made from a single rectangle of material.

Bark fibres can be used for true weaving, as was done by some American Indians, but they are not as satisfactory as other vegetable fibres such as flax, hemp and cotton. These, however, require cultivation and are therefore little used by nomadic people in the pastoral stage. Such people had sheep, and wool seems to have been employed in the Neolithic period. In the New World the useful animals were the llama, the alpaca and the vicuña.

Weaving on any extensive scale requires a fixed abode, since a loom tends to be large and heavy and therefore difficult to transport from place to place. The ideal situation for development was a small, settled community surrounded by grazing lands for sheep. The fleece was clipped off by methods closely

5 Assurbanipal II from Nimrud. Babylonian, 883–859 B C. Male costume consisting of a long tunic with close-fitting sleeves. The diagonal fringes of the skirt are formed by a shawl thrown over one shoulder

6 Persian tribute-bearer from Persepolis, fifth century B C. The feet are booted, and the headdress is formed of a band of material

resembling those in use today; the resultant bunch of fibre was then spun off and the thread woven into cloth on a loom. Once cloth manufacture, on however small a scale, had been established, the way was open for the development of costume as we know it.

The simplest method of using cloth for what is significantly termed 'clothing' was to wrap a small rectangle of it round the waist, thus making a sarong, the primitive form of the skirt. Later, another square of cloth was draped over the

12

7 Persian archers from Susa, fifth–fourth century BC. Tunics made of patterned material, belted and with wide sleeves. The hair and beards were curled by means of hot tongs

shoulders and kept in place by fibulae. Clothing of this nature was used by the Egyptians, the Assyrians, the Greeks and the Romans. In fact draped clothes were the mark of civilization. Tailored clothes were regarded as 'barbarian' and the Romans at one time went so far as to decree the death penalty for wearing them.

Draped clothes plainly required a considerable development in the art of weaving in order to produce rectangles of cloth large enough for the purpose. The transition from skins of beasts to woven cloth was not, however, as simple or as immediate as was once supposed. Statuettes and bas-reliefs of the ancient Sumerian civilization of Mesopotamia (third millennium B C) show figures wearing skirts composed of tufted
Ills. 2–4 tissues: that is, cloth which presents the appearance of tufts of wool arranged symmetrically, sometimes as a series of flounces. Once the tufts, or independent strands, were relegated to the borders of the cloth rectangles, they became a fringe, and this vestigial element can be seen very plainly in almost all the garments worn by Assyrians and Babylonians of both sexes.

It has been pointed out that the fringed shawls (for that would seem the most rewarding way to think of them) com-
Ill. 5 posing the costume of, for example, Assurbanipal, as seen in his statue in the British Museum, are shown much more tightly draped about the body than could have been the case in real life. The sculptor has eliminated all folds and wrinkles in order to portray more clearly the patterns of the figured cloth.

Women and high dignitaries continued to wear garments of this kind, but they were gradually replaced in ordinary male costume by a kind of tunic with sleeves. It is thought that the sleeves were due to the influence of the mountain people round about, as were also the closed boots. Both would seem to have been unnecessary in the very hot climate of the Euphrates and the Tigris valleys.

Women are seldom represented in the bas-reliefs found at Nineveh, although they are rich in representations of male costume. There are, however, certain statues of goddesses which show them in long, flounced robes. It is interesting to note that an Assyrian law of about 1200 B C compelled married women to wear veils in public, the earliest record of a custom which has prevailed in these districts until modern times. The hair was worn long by both sexes. Hair and beards were curled and sometimes interwoven with gold thread. Men's headgear was in the shape of an inverted flower-pot, although warriors, of course, wore helmets, terminating in a kind of blunt spike. Protective clothing was at first of leather, later covered, for the heavy infantry and cavalry, with metal plaques.

The Persians overran the Babylonian civilization in the sixth century B C. Since they came from the colder climate of the mountains of what is now called Turkistan, they wore warmer clothes but soon abandoned these for the fringed tunics and overmantles of the conquered race. In addition to wool and linen they now had access to silk, brought from China by the *Ill. 7* long caravan route. They retained, however, their characteristic headdress, the soft felt cap which the Greeks called 'Phrygian' and which, some two thousand years later, was adopted by the French revolutionaries as 'the red cap of Liberty'. *Ill. 6* They also kept their characteristic footgear, a closed boot of supple leather slightly turned up at the toe. The most important innovation was the wearing of trousers, which came to be looked upon as the typical Persian garment and, if we can rely on the very scanty records available, were probably worn by women also.

The Medes who shared in the Persian conquests were of the same race and wore similar garments, but looser and more voluminous. The headdresses also were different, consisting either of a round cap with a flat crown or of a hood. There was little contrast in male and female costume except that the women's coats were wider and longer. But it would be profitless, within the limits of this brief survey, to attempt to establish minor differences in costume between Persians and Medes, and the still semi-nomadic people, such as the Scythians, the Dacians and the Sarmatians of the neighbouring steppes.

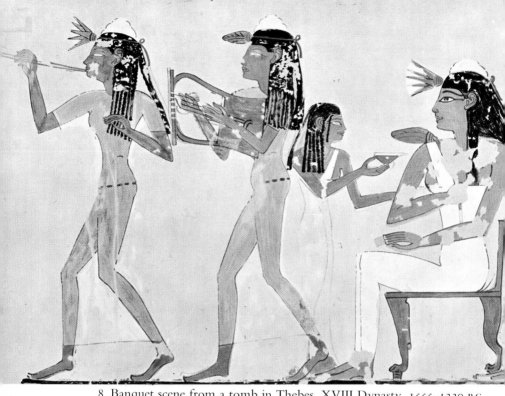

8 Banquet scene from a tomb in Thebes, XVIII Dynasty, 1555–1330 BC.
The dancers wear bead girdles, which are plainly visible through the
diaphanous material of the long tunic – an early example of the 'see-through'
dress

The valley of the Nile is no hotter than the valley of the
Euphrates, but Egyptian costume was much scantier and lighter
than that of Assyria and Babylon. Indeed, many of the lower
Ill. 8 classes, and the slaves in the palaces, went about almost, if not
completely, naked. The wearing of clothes was a kind of
class distinction.

Fortunately, we know a great deal about Ancient Egyptian
dress, from statuettes and wall-paintings, which, owing to the
extremely dry climate, have been preserved in enormous
numbers. The available documentation is greater than that of
any other ancient civilization, and the most striking thing
about it is its static quality. Over a period of nearly three
thousand years the changes to be noted are minimal.

16

9 Tutankhamen and his queen, XVIII Dynasty, 1350–1340 BC. Royal
costume differed from that of other Egyptians by being of finer material,
with embroidered belts and collars of gold and enamel

During what is called the Old Kingdom (i.e. before 1500 BC) the characteristic garment was the *schenti*, a piece of woven material used as a loin-cloth and kept in place by a belt. For *Ill. 11* kings and dignitaries it was pleated and stiffened and sometimes embroidered. Under the New Kingdom (1500 BC to 332 BC) the Pharaohs also wore a long, fringed tunic called a *kalasiris*, which, being semi-transparent, allowed the loin-cloth to be seen underneath. It was made of a rectangular piece of material and was sometimes woven in one piece, producing, when worn by women, a tight-fitting garment finishing below the breasts and kept in place by shoulder straps. (The extremely *Ill. 10* tight-fitting appearance of women's clothes in sculpture and painting is probably due to the conventions of Egyptian art; the actual garments were almost certainly more ample.) A short cape sometimes covered the shoulders, or else the throat was encircled with a wide, jewelled collar, leaving the breasts exposed.

Unlike other ancient peoples the Egyptians made little use of wool, since animal fibres were considered impure. After the Alexandrian conquest, it came to be used in the fabrication of ordinary garments but was still forbidden in the dress of priests and in burial clothes. For these the finest linen was required.

The Ancient Egyptians had extremely high standards of hygiene, and one of the advantages of fine linen garments was that they could be easily washed. For similar reasons men shaved their heads and wore a headdress made of a square of striped material encircling the temples and forming square pleats over the ears. On ceremonial occasions, wigs were worn, sometimes made of natural hair, sometimes of flax or palm-fibre. Such wigs have been found in early tombs, and the custom of wearing them lasted for thousands of years.

The young princesses shown in frescoes also had shaven heads, but mature women generally wore their own hair, sometimes frizzed or waved. The Egyptians wore no hats. What we see on the heads of the Pharaohs is a crown, or rather two crowns, 'the crown of the North and the crown of the

10 Woman bearing offerings, XI–XII Dynasty, *c.* 2000 B C. The patterning on the tight-fitting dress is thought to have been composed of a coloured network of leather

11 King Akenaton and Queen Nefertite, XVIII Dynasty, 1555–1330 B C. The King wears the *schenti* or loin-cloth of fine pleated material, the Queen the long tunic, or *haik*, fastened at the waist. Both have deep collars of beads and jewels

South', one in the form of a circlet and the other in the form of a conical helmet. A protective metal helmet was, of course, worn by warriors. After the Greek conquest, Egyptian costume gradually became modified by foreign influences, although the extreme conservatism of the Egyptians preserved the ancient modes at least for ceremonial and religious ceremonies.

19

12, 14 Left and right, snake goddesses from the Palace of Knossos, Crete, c. 1600 B C

13 Above, *La Parisienne*. Fresco from Knossos, Crete, 1550–1450 B C

There is a curious modernity about these figures. With their tight waists and skirts *à la Polonaise* they suggest French fashions of the 1870s

Before we discuss 'classical' costume, however, it is necessary to consider the surprising clothes worn in Crete before the *Ills. 12–14* collapse of the Minoan civilization about the year 1400 B C. The very existence of this civilization was hardly suspected until the excavations of Sir Arthur Evans at the beginning of the present century revealed the richness of its artefacts and the elaboration of its clothes.

Crete seems to have been inhabited before the sixth millennium B C, but it was not until the beginning of the third millennium that a wave of immigrants from the Cyclades

21

introduced a skill in navigation which enabled them to trade with Egypt and Asia Minor. It was inevitable that both these centres should influence the Cretans; but, at least from about 2000 BC, they developed a national style of striking originality.

From the costume point of view the most interesting period is the three and a half centuries which stretched from 1750 BC to 1400 BC. It was during this time that the Palace of Knossos was constructed, and it was from the excavations conducted there that most of our information is derived. The documentation consists of frescoes, painted pots and statuettes. Of these the last category is the most important, for the pots are not very numerous (compared with the large quantity that have come down to us from the 'classical' Greek period), and the frescoes are, naturally enough, in a poor state of repair and have not always been judiciously restored. With the clay figurines, however, we are on firm ground and they reveal an astonishing degree of luxury and refinement.

In a sense, of course, they are 'primitive' clothes in that male
Ill. 15 costume consists essentially of a loin-cloth, leaving the torso bare. Female costume shows a series of flounces with a tightly nipped-in waist and a corsage which terminates below the breasts. But the form of the male loin-cloth was much more varied than that of the Egyptian *schenti* and could consist of linen, wool or leather. For women the primitive loin-cloth had been lengthened to reach the ground and, by superimposing one piece of material over another, an effect was produced strangely similar to some of the European fashions of the late nineteenth century. The extremely tight waist accentuates this resemblance, and the result is so *chic*, in the modern sense, that one of the most attractive of the figures shown in the frescoes
Ill. 13 has been nicknamed *La Parisienne*.

The belts worn by men were sometimes adorned with metal plaques and sometimes made entirely of metal. The extreme slimness of the waist suggests that they were worn from early childhood. The metals used were gold, silver and bronze, and the belts composed of them are sometimes richly chased. In general men went bare-headed, although a kind of turban or bonnet was sometimes worn. Women, on the other hand, had the most elaborate headdresses, the hair being arranged in a variety of ways and surmounted by what may perhaps be regarded as the first 'smart hats' in the history of costume. Some of them are a curious anticipation of the hats worn by the Tanagra figurines of the Age of Pericles.   *Ill. 16*

The Cretans had a passion for bright colours such as red, yellow, blue and purple, as can be seen quite plainly in the frescoes that have been preserved. They were also extremely fond of jewellery, quantities of which have been discovered in the tombs of both men and women: rings, bracelets, collars, hair-pins. Rich people wore necklaces of lapis lazuli, agate, amethyst and rock-crystal mingled with pearls. The less widespread use of fibulae is not surprising: as opposed to draped Greek clothes, Cretan clothes were both cut to shape and draped, thus requiring less pinning. It is the former 'classical' garments which we must now consider.

15 Priest-king from Knossos, Crete, 1550–1450 BC. Cretan men as well as women show the extremely constricted waist which could only have been attained by wearing a rigid girdle from childhood

16 Lady from Tanagra (right) and maid-servant from Alexandria, third century
B C. Over a tunic or *chiton*, women wore an enveloping mantle of linen or wool
similar to the male *himation*. The curious little hat worn by the lady was probably
made of plaited straw

CHAPTER TWO

Greeks and Romans

S CHOLARS now realize that the old 'classical' picture of Greece was much too simple. It was indeed bound to be so before the discovery of the Cretan civilization. It is true none the less that, from the period of the Dorian invasions of about 1200 BC, a new culture emerged which in manners and costume showed itself remarkably stable. Until the time of Alexander, in fact, there was no essential modification in the clothes worn by men or by women.

Greek costume during this long period had no form in itself. It was composed of rectangles of cloth of various sizes draped over the body without cutting or sewing the material. There could, of course, be considerable variation in the manner of adjustment, but the essential lines remained the same.

From the seventh to the first century B C both men and women wore the *chiton*, knee-length for men, ankle-length for women. Men, however, sometimes wore it long, as can be seen from the famous statue known as the 'Charioteer of Delphi'. It was *Ill. 18* kept in place by pins or brooches and was usually worn with a cord or belt round the waist. Scholars distinguish between the Doric and the Ionic *chiton*, the former being generally made of wool and the latter of linen. This being a more flexible material, it allowed a greater variety of folds, and the oblong of linen used was sometimes longer than the distance between the shoulders and the feet, enabling the cloth to be drawn up under the belt to form a kind of blouse.

It was at one time supposed that Greek clothes were white or of the natural colour of wool or flax, but this error derived from the fact that the antique statues discovered during the Renaissance had lost any colour they might have possessed. Further researches have shown that Greek garments were often

25

coloured and patterned, except presumably those worn by the poor.

Some members of the lower classes dyed their garments a reddish brown, a practice apparently disapproved of by the authorities, for the historian Herodotus mentions an Athenian decree forbidding them to appear in dyed clothes at the theatre and in other public places. The upper classes were allowed more liberty, and it is said that the painter Polygnotus was the first to introduce brilliant colours such as red, yellow and purple. A polychrome statue recently discovered shows traces of green. The decoration of garments, often confined to the border, was embroidered rather than woven into the cloth and consisted of formal patterns such as the 'Greek fret', flowers and animal figures.

17 The goddess Athena, c. 450 BC. Greek costume was essentially drapery, a large rectangle of wool or linen being adjusted in various ways and held in place by one or two girdles, and by fibulae at the point of the shoulder

18 The Charioteer of Delphi, c. 475 BC. The long tunic or *chiton* was worn by both men and women, although for men it was a ceremonial garment, the short *chiton* being worn in ordinary life

19, 20 Outline drawings of bas reliefs of the fifth century B C

21 Right, maenad dancing. Roman copy of Greek original, late fifth century B C

All these show the different ways in which the rectangle of cloth could be adjusted round the body

The essential garment, the *chiton*, being a simple rectangle of cloth folded round the body, could be adjusted in various ways. Men could either fasten it with a brooch or pin on the left shoulder, leaving the right bare, or it could be fastened on both shoulders. It could be worn with one cord or belt round the waist or with two. No belt at all was worn before putting on a breastplate over it. In its later form the *chiton* was made of two pieces of cloth sewn together and was sometimes provided with sleeves.

Young men in general, and horsemen in particular, wore over the *chiton* a kind of short cloak, usually fastened on one

Ill. 23   shoulder and known as a *chlamys*. There was no impropriety in wearing the *chlamys* only, without the *chiton*, and in the gymnasium both sexes exercised naked: that, in fact, is what the word 'gymnasium' means. The Greeks, unlike their Semitic contemporaries, did not regard nudity as shameful. In cold weather a much larger cloak was worn: the *himation*. It could

24 Girl from Verona, Italy. Roman copy of a Greek original, 50 BC–AD 50. A later, more sophisticated Greek costume, including a *chlamydon* made from a rectangle of cloth, slit to pass over the head. The soft fabric is held in gathers by a cord passing under the left breast

22 Far left, torso of the goddess Minerva, mid fifth century BC

23 Left, boy wearing a *chlamys*, the short military cloak consisting, in this case, of a circular piece of material kept in place by a brooch on the right shoulder. Roman copy of Greek original of the first century BC

measure as much as eight feet by six. The female form of the *chlamys* was known as the *peplos* and, like its male counterpart, was worn over the *chiton*, which reached to the woman's feet. As luxury increased, it was sometimes made of very fine material, even of silk, in spite of repeated sumptuary laws which endeavoured to restrain the luxury of female garments. *Ill. 24* It should perhaps be noted here that luxury does not imply 'fashion'. The respectable Athenian lady was rarely seen abroad and had little temptation to compete with other women in striking or novel garments.

31

25 Head of an unknown woman from Sicily, sixth century BC, showing regional variation or possibly Egyptian influence

26 Head of the Muse Polyhymnia. Roman copy of Hellenistic original

27 Head of the Borghese Hera. Probably Roman copy of Greek original, third century BC

In the styles of hairdressing, however, we can trace considerable developments over the centuries. Before the Greek victories against the Persians, both men and women wore their hair long. Later, long hair was considered suitable only for boys or women. At puberty a boy cut off his hair and dedicated it to the gods.

Even before the middle of the fifth century BC women sometimes bound their hair with a fillet. Afterwards this became the usual practice, and the back hair was sometimes *Ill. 27* enclosed in a kind of chignon worn low on the nape of the neck. Later still the back hair was fastened with ribbons in the form of a cone projecting behind the head. Wealthy women wore tiaras of gold and precious stones, and, after the Roman conquest, hair-styles became much more numerous and elaborate, with much use of frizzing and curling and the addition of artificial hair. Hats were used only for travelling, and even then were frequently worn on the shoulder rather than on the head. They were made of felt and had very broad brims. However, the Tanagra statuettes show that after the Mace-

32

donian conquest many women wore comical little hats, rather *Ill. 16*
like a miniature version of a Chinese hat, perched on the top
of their heads.

In general the Greeks were bearded up to the fifth century
BC, and even after that philosophers and other serious persons
kept up the old usage. Younger men shaved off all facial hair,
and the younger gods like Apollo and Mercury are always
depicted clean-shaven, the older ones like Jupiter and Vulcan
retaining their beards.

Indoors the Greeks rarely wore footgear of any kind, and the
poorer classes went barefoot even in the street. Even wealthy
people wore only sandals, although those of the courtesans
were sometimes gilded, the soles being studded with nails
arranged in such a way as to leave a footprint spelling out the
words 'Follow me'. (Such a sandal has actually been preserved.
It was found in Lower Egypt, but is thought by scholars to
have been similar to those worn by Greek courtesans.) The
sandals were attached to the feet and ankles by thongs tied in
many different ways, as innumerable statues testify.

28, 29 Warriors from vase-paintings, fifth century BC

Both figures are in armour, worn over the short tunic. The helmet of the second figure is the more characteristic. The shield, seen from the back, shows the method of holding it

The artists of the classical revival in the late eighteenth and early nineteenth centuries were persuaded – no doubt by the numerous nude statues in museums – that the Ancient Greeks went into battle naked, armed only with a sword, a shield and a helmet. In reality the Greek warriors protected themselves *Ill. 28* with tunics of leather reinforced with metal plaques, and wore greaves on their legs. The heavily armed infantry – the hoplites – and the cavalry wore in addition the characteristic Greek helmet which almost enclosed the head. It was sometimes provided with movable side pieces but had no visor, being *Ill. 29* merely pushed back on the head when not in use. The crest took the form of a horse's mane and was usually made of horsehair. The effect was singularly striking and beautiful. The light infantry wore greaves of leather and tunics of doubled felt or leather with a metal belt. They also wore the *chlamys*, fastened on the shoulder or, in battle, rolled round the left arm to parry blows.

Just as archaeology has destroyed the long-accepted picture of Greek history, it has also modified our opinions of life during the first millennium B C in the Italian peninsula. So much was known of the Roman civilization that it was hardly realized how long a time elapsed before Rome became anything more than one small city-state struggling against its neighbours for survival and finally for dominance. Everybody knew that Rome had a king called Tarquin, but the implications of this were not so generally grasped: that the Romans at an early period of their development were ruled by a foreign dynasty, that of the Etruscans.

Who were the Etruscans? Scholars are still divided in their opinions. They are thought by some to have migrated from Asia, perhaps in successive waves, between the thirteenth and the eighth centuries BC. Others have thought that they represented an ethnic group of even earlier origin. They had connections with both Greece and Asia Minor and their costume reflects both influences. Of this costume there is now a considerable documentation, mostly in the form of statues and bas-reliefs. Moreover, little as we know about their literature or their language, their recently discovered sculpture and wall-paintings enable us to reconstruct a fairly comprehensive picture of their mode of life.

Until their expansion into the southern part of Italy brought the Etruscans into contact with the Greek colonies of Magna Graecia, their garments showed little trace of Greek influence. Rather, they reflected an earlier connection with the Cretan civilization modified by Oriental elements: their clothes were both sewn and draped. We can trace a certain evolution from *Ill. 30* what the scholars call a 'tunic-robe', characteristic of the period from about 700 BC to 575 BC, to a kind of toga made (like the

30 An Etruscan female dancer, end of sixth century BC, wearing a sewn garment

31 Dancers from the Tomb of the Leopards, Tarquinia. Etruscan, first
quarter of fifth century BC

Roman toga which was derived from it) of a semicircle of cloth.   *Ill. 31*
Sometimes it was rectangular and formed a kind of cloak. This
was worn by men, while women wore a long, tight-fitting
robe, without a girdle, with half-sleeves and sometimes slit at
the back, closed by ribbons when the garment had been put on
over the head. Over the robe was worn a long, rectangular
cloak which, when required, could be drawn over the head.

The most striking difference between Greek and Etruscan
costume was in the footwear. Until the fifth century BC, when
Greek influences caused them to adopt sandals, the Etruscans
wore a kind of high, laced boot with a turned-up toe, which was
obviously derived from the footwear of Asia Minor. But the
whole question of reciprocal influences is a field of study as yet
only partially explored. Once the Romans had established their
hegemony over the whole of Italy, they imposed their own way
of life and costume, and the very memory of a previous
Etruscan civilization faded away.

As we have seen, however, the Romans borrowed from the Etruscans one garment which became characteristically their own: the toga. In its Roman form it grew ever more voluminous, required considerable skill in draping it about the body and effectively prevented any active pursuit. It was therefore essentially a garment for the upper classes, especially for senators, with whom it was always white. Until they attained puberty, free-born boys wore it with a purple border, when it was known as a *toga praetexta*, to be ceremonially exchanged for a white *toga virilis* when the time came. In mourning, a dark-coloured toga was worn and was sometimes draped over the head, as it was also for certain religious ceremonies. After about A D 100 the toga began to diminish in size, shrinking first to a *pallium* and then to a mere band of cloth, the stole. In the early days of the Republic, men wore a simple loin-cloth made of

Ills. 32, 33

32 Opposite, Vestal virgin. Roman, second century A D. On ceremonial occasions or in mourning a fold of cloth was drawn over the head

33 The Emperor Tiberius, first century A D. The Emperor is wearing the toga over a sleeved tunic

linen, this being replaced under the Empire by a sewn tunic, the equivalent of the Greek *chiton*. It consisted of two pieces of cloth sewn together, was put on over the head and gathered at the waist by means of a belt. It was knee-length, except on special occasions such as weddings, when it reached to the ground. It was worn under the toga by the upper classes; soldiers and workmen wore it as their sole garment. When provided with elbow-length sleeves it was known as a 'dalmatic', the name it continued to bear when, in a slightly modified form, it became one of the vestments of the Christian

39

Church. When it was embroidered all over it was called a *tunica palmata*. In pagan times it was worn, a little longer than knee-length, by the Roman dandies.

Sometimes two tunics were worn, the one next to the skin being the *subacula* and the over-tunic the *tunica exteriodum*. The latter grew gradually longer, reaching to the ankles from about AD 100. It was then known as a *caracalla*, and by AD 200 had been adopted by almost everyone.

At first the Romans, with their hardy traditions, strongly disapproved both of trews (to use the Scottish term) and of the long trousers worn by the barbarian tribes. But they gradually became accepted, being adopted first by soldiers.

At first the Romans were bearded, but from the second century BC they began to be clean-shaven, and this became the universal custom under the Empire until the time of Hadrian, who once more introduced beards. Hair was worn short, which

34 'Bikini girl' from Sicily, late third century AD. The Romans, unlike the Greeks, did not exercise in the gymnasium naked, but wore a modicum of clothing very similar to modern styles

35 Statues of the first century A D showing varieties of drapery. Centre, a priest offering a libation, with a fold of the toga drawn over his head

did not preclude considerable luxury, the dandies having their locks curled by means of hot tongs. In general the head was uncovered, but felt hats of various forms were sometimes worn: the rimless cap known as the *pileus*, a hat with a wide brim copied from the Greeks, and the soft Phrygian bonnet. The *cuculus* was a type of hood, sometimes attached to the cloak and sometimes forming a separate garment.

Women's clothes were at first very similar to those worn by men except for an unstiffened kind of bust-bodice known as the *strophium*. The tunic, however, was much longer than the masculine variety and formed a robe reaching to the feet. It was made first of wool, then of linen or cotton and finally, for the wealthy, of silk. The favourite colours were red, yellow and blue, and the garment was sometimes ornamented with a gold fringe and lavishly embroidered.

Ill. 34

41

36–9 Four heads showing the growing elaboration of hair-styles in the Roman period. Left, head of matron or widow. Right, Greek style

The *stola*, worn over the tunic, was a garment of similar shape but with sleeves, and over this was draped, for out of doors, a voluminous cloak, rather like the toga but rectangular in shape, known as the *pella*. In public it was usual for the head to be veiled. Hairdressing gradually grew more elaborate, and from the time of Messalina onwards it was impossible for a fashionable lady to dispense with the services of an *ornatrix*, who spent hours arranging the locks in a cone called a *tutulus* or surrounding the face with a frame of tight curls. Blonde hair was fashionable and, as we learn from Ovid, those who were naturally dark-haired resorted to bleaches. There was much use of false hair and even of entire wigs. The innumerable portrait-busts surviving from the later Empire show an enormous variety of styles, and it is evidence of the rapid changing of fashion that some ladies had their heads sculptured in two pieces so that the upper part, representing the hair, could be replaced, if desired, by a more fashionable coiffure.

Ills. 36–9

42

Left, head showing Egyptian influence. Hellenistic. Right, head of a woman of the Flavian period, second century A D

All this was part of an increasing luxury, which satirists such as Juvenal seized upon as evidence of national decline. Jewellery of all kinds was increasingly worn. Simple head-bands were replaced by gold and silver tiaras encrusted with precious stones and cameos. Rings were worn by both sexes; the women added bracelets, anklets, necklaces and ear-rings. The poet Ovid mentions ear-rings made of three rows of pearls. Use was made of enamels and damascening, of ivory and cameos. Many of these artefacts came to Rome as the result of its conquests. Antioch and Alexandria were the principal centres of manufacture, but by the time of Augustus many articles were being made in Rome itself.

Decoration even spread to footwear, although this had originally been extremely simple: a sandal made of a single piece of untanned hide, overlapping the outline of the foot and kept in place by leather thongs. This was known as the *carbatina*, and in its slightly more sophisticated form as the *calceus*, and

43

was worn by the majority of Roman citizens. Slaves were forbidden to use it. Indoors women wore a kind of slipper called the *soccus*, which could be of various colours and was sometimes painted with patterns and even studded with precious stones after the manner of the *calceus patricius* worn by the Emperor Nero. Buskins, or closed boots, were sometimes used in bad weather. They were called *gallicae*, which is sufficient evidence that they had been borrowed from the Gauls.

Foreign influences of all kinds became more marked with the expansion of the Empire, especially with its expansion towards the east, until there was no luxury which the Roman patricians could not, if they wished, adopt. And then the centre of government itself moved east, with the establishment by Constantine of a new capital on the Bosphorus: Constantinople. And a new chapter opened in the history of Roman costume.

There had been a colony of Greeks on the European side of the Bosphorus since the seventh century BC, but for a thousand

40 Sarcophagus, late fourth century AD. The togas worn by these Christian Romans are markedly less ample than in previous centuries

41 Procession of female saints from Ravenna. Byzantine, *c.* 561

years it was little more than a military centre with primitive fortifications. Then, in AD 330, the Emperor Constantine founded Constantinople on the site as his new capital. However, it did not long remain the capital of the whole Empire, which was divided after the death of Theodosius the Great in AD 395 into the Eastern and Western Empires.

When the Western Empire fell in AD 476, Byzantium, or Constantinople as it was now called, was cut off from the West and became more and more affected by those Oriental influences which had been felt from its foundation. It could hardly have been otherwise, for its position made it the natural entrepôt of trade with the interior of Asia.

This naturally resulted in the evolution of quite a different kind of costume, a change neatly summed up by Carolyn G. *Ill. 41* Bradley: 'The simplicity of the old Roman dress gave way to the gay coloring, fringes, tassels and jewels of the East. The

45

idea in dress in this era was to conceal and obscure the body'
(*Western World Costume*, New York 1954). Constantine himself wore a costume very different from that of earlier Roman
emperors. His robe of gold tissue was embroidered with floral
patterns. Fastened to his shoulder by a jewelled brooch was a
purple *chlamys*. A wide scarf called a *trabea* was crossed on his
chest. The tunic had narrow sleeves, sometimes replaced by
the wide-sleeved dalmatic, both encrusted with jewels as was
also the *tablion*, an oblong panel on the front of the garment.
Round his head he wore a band of material knotted at the
back, but later emperors substituted a kind of crown, set with
jewels and with strings of gems hanging from it on either side.
This can be seen quite plainly in the splendid mosaics in the
Ills. 42–4   church of San Vitale in Ravenna. These show, in an elaborate
frieze, the figures of the Emperor Justinian and his wife Theodora and are among the most valuable documents we possess
of Byzantine costume at the height of its glory in the sixth
century.

One is struck at once by the *ecclesiastical* look of the Imperial
garments. The Emperor was indeed a priest-king, the Viceroy
of Christ on Earth. He did not actually say Mass, but he incensed
the altar at sacred ceremonies, and it was he who called the
Councils of the Church and, in some cases, presided over them.
His whole life was regulated by liturgical requirements, all laid
down with meticulous care in the *Book of Ceremonies* and,
whenever he appeared in public, his clothes were not so much
garments as 'vestments'. Similarly, the dress of all the courtiers
and palace attendants was rigidly laid down in accordance with
rank and function. In Byzantium as in Imperial China, all
dress was 'hierarchical'. The 'Seduction Principle' was almost
entirely absent, and the 'Utility Principle' completely ignored.

If, however, the Emperor was a priest-king he was also an
Oriental potentate, a late echo of Darius 'King of Kings' and
an early anticipation of the Turkish sultans who were later to
rule in Constantinople. His palace was a strange mixture of
monastery and seraglio, swarming with monks and eunuchs.

46

Another Oriental touch was the method of selecting an Empress. It resolved itself into a kind of beauty competition, girls being brought from every part of the Empire. Their rank does not seem to have mattered, and when the candidates had been screened and only the most beautiful remained, the Emperor himself made the final choice, presenting the girl with an apple. Fantastic as it may seem, it was in this manner that Justinian selected Theodora. She was of humble origin, her father being in charge of the bears used in bear-baiting. But in Theodora's case there was another difficulty: she was an actress and dancer, professions of which the Church strongly disapproved. Special legislation had to be enacted in order to allow her to marry Justinian.

Once elevated to the purple, she showed herself a woman of great courage and indomitable will. She made an admirable consort. She was, of course, surrounded by all the ecclesiastical pomp that surrounded her husband, and her appearance, like his, is preserved for posterity in the gleaming mosaics of San Vitale. She wore a long white tunic adorned with a vertical band covered with embroideries. Another band, called a *maniakis*, embroidered with gold thread and set with precious stones and pearls, was draped over her shoulders. In addition she wore a short-sleeved robe, with a jewelled belt and fringes at the hem, and a purple cloak embroidered with figures of the Magi. On her head she had an even more splendid diadem than the Emperor's. This was the *stephanos*, set with precious stones and with long strings of pearls hanging down on either side. On her feet were closed shoes of soft leather, coloured red and enriched with embroideries.

The materials used were rich and varied, as may be gathered from the fragments that have survived, mostly as ecclesiastical vestments or the wrappings of relics. Wool, which had been the textile most in use in the early days of the Empire, was laid aside in favour of cotton and fine linens from Egypt and silk from China. The latter had at first to be transported by caravan across the whole width of Asia, a lengthy and costly business.

47

Ill. 44

And then, according to the legend, two missionary monks were dispatched by Theodora herself to China and returned bringing with them a number of silkworms in a hollow cane. This, perhaps, is the first example in history of industrial espionage. In any case, the silkworms flourished and multiplied and Byzantium was able to spin and weave its own silk cloth.

The most striking thing about the costume of New Rome as opposed to that of Old Rome was its colour. Purple was reserved for the Imperial couple but all other colours were employed in the clothes of the rich. Many garments were heavily patterned with animals, flowers and Biblical scenes. It is recorded that one Byzantine senator had on his toga a complete series of pictures representing the life of Christ. This emphasizes once more the close connection, unknown perhaps at any other period of history, between ecclesiastical and civil costume.

It is impossible to record here all the modifications which occurred in Byzantine costume over the centuries. It is sufficient to note that they nearly all provide evidence of increasing Orientalization. In the twelfth century the Persian *caftan* was adopted, as well as a mantle buttoned down the front. The open coronet of Justinian was exchanged for a closed crown called a *camelaukion*. From Assyria was derived the long-sleeved *granatza*, a robe reaching to the ground. From the sixth century turbans were sometimes worn, and scholars have noted, between the seventh and ninth centuries, a Chinese influence on hats.

But if Byzantine costume was affected by foreign influences, it in its turn was much imitated in surrounding districts. Even after the fall of Constantinople, Bulgarian kings wore clothes of Byzantine derivation and the rulers of Muscovy continued to do so until the seventeenth century, when Peter the Great broke with tradition and turned Russia's face to the West. And, of course, the Orthodox Church continues to this day to perform its ceremonies in vestments not essentially different from those worn by the Byzantine emperors.

48

42–44 Byzantine splendour: the Empress Theodora and her suite, 500–526.
Above left, Theodora's husband, the Emperor Justinian

CHAPTER THREE

Early Europe

THROUGHOUT its history the Roman State was surrounded
by barbarian peoples who lived beyond the borders of its
dominion, and sometimes their incursions were dangerous
indeed. As early as the second century BC, a Roman army had
been defeated by a people they identified as Teutoni or Teutons.

At this period the Teutons were primitive enough. Their
principal garment seems to have consisted of a short tunic
formed of two pieces of leather sewn together. Later it was
made of wool or linen. Under the tunic were worn breeches or
baggy trousers, which in Roman eyes was the very mark of the
barbarian. Naturally, the Teutons were influenced by their
contacts with Rome, and they gradually adopted something
resembling Roman costume but made, in general, of coarser
materials such as hemp.

By the end of the first century AD, another northern tribe, the
Goths (originally of Scandinavian origin), had settled in what
was, until 1945, East Prussia, and they, too, threatened the
Roman civilization. They sacked Rome under their great leader
Alaric in the fifth century. As Ostrogoths they pushed south into
central Italy; as Visigoths they pushed westward into Spain and
other regions; and as Langobards or Lombards they firmly established themselves in northern Italy. From the descriptions of
such Roman historians as Sidonius Apollinaris we know that
they wore sleeved tunics of linen, edged with fur, and became
gradually Romanized.

New waves of invasion from the east threatened the Teutonic
tribes themselves. The Huns came originally from Mongolia;
by the middle of the first century AD they had reached Europe,
and by the fourth century, under Attila, Rome itself.

In France the Gauls had adopted not only Roman dress and customs but the Latin language. Like the Britons they had (in the upper classes at least) become completely Romanized. But Gaul was successfully invaded by the Franks (i.e. the Teutons) from across the Rhine, and by the fifth century A D the Frankish dynasty of the Merovingians had established itself over the greater part of the country.

We would know much less of the costume of the Merovingian period in France (A D 481–752) if it were not for the fact that the invading Franks who now controlled the country were in the habit of burying their dead, instead of burning their bodies as the Romanized Gauls had done. Buried with the corpses of kings or other distinguished persons were the clothes, arms and accoutrements they had used in life. Excavations in Lorraine and at Le Mans have yielded specimens of fine linen garments which, although fragmentary, show that it was usual to wear a knee-length tunic called a *gonelle*, embroidered at the edge and caught in at the waist with a belt. In battle the tunic would be made of stout material, or of leather, and covered with metal plaques. The men of this period wore *braies* or breeches, sometimes ending at the knee and leaving the legs bare, sometimes long and cross-gartered.

Little is known of female costume at this period, since women are poorly represented in the burials. We know, however, from other sources, that they generally wore a long tunic called a *stola* decorated with embroidered bands. The arms were bare. Brooches kept the garment in place on the shoulders, and the waist was encircled with a leather belt. A kind of scarf, called a *palla*, was draped over the shoulders.

Fortunately, one quite recent discovery, in the church of Saint-Denis, near Paris, gives more exact information. Fragments of material from the tomb of a Merovingian queen, Arnegonde (A D 550–70), show that she was buried in a chemise of fine linen with a violet silk robe over it. Over this was a long tunic of red silk, open in front and with long wide sleeves. A wide belt, crossed at the back and tied low in front, kept the tunic in place, and attached to the tunic by richly enamelled gold fibulae was a waist-length veil. The closed shoes were of black leather with laces long enough to be crossed over the leg to the height of the garter.

Neither men nor women seem to have worn hats. Both sexes had long hair, men and young girls wearing it loose, and married women binding it into a kind of chignon. The latter covered the head with a veil, either in the form of a turban or long enough to cover the entire body.

When the Merovingians were succeeded by the Carolingians (AD 752–987), conditions in France and in Western Europe generally were rather more settled and luxury increased. Charlemagne became ruler of the Franks, controlling, in AD 771, territory corresponding roughly to France and Germany; and in AD 800 he was crowned in Rome as Emperor. We have a detailed description of his costume from the hand of his secretary Eginhard, but we must be careful to distinguish between his ordinary dress and the clothes he felt compelled to wear as Roman Emperor. The latter were of extreme magnificence and were plainly derived from the Court dress of Byzantium. This was not only a matter of cut: the actual materials were almost certainly imported from the Near East. Fragments are still preserved of the clothes in which he was buried at Aachen and we have records of the complete garments found when his tomb was opened in the twelfth century.

Over a tunic with sleeves edged with gold he wore a dalmatic, and over this a number of garments, including one of brocade manufactured in Constantinople, figured with elephants in floriated circles of green, blue and gold, and one of cloth-of-gold, brocaded in squares with a ruby in the centre of each. His shoes were of scarlet leather embroidered with gold and set with emeralds. On his head he wore a splendid gold crown set with jewels and enamelled plaques.

Eginhard tells us that his habitual costume was much simpler, consisting of an under-tunic of linen or wool and over it a tunic with a border of coloured silk. Over this again he wore,

45 The four parts of the Empire (Sclavinia, Germania, Gallia and Roma) paying homage to Otto III; right, the Emperor Otto enthroned, 997–1000. The miniature shows the bright colours worn in the period

attached to his left shoulder by means of a brooch, a short semi-circular cloak, lined with fur in winter. He had *braies* or breeches cross-gartered to below the knee, and on his head a round cloth cap with an embroidered border.

In England, Charlemagne's contemporary, Offa, King of Mercia, and the kings who followed him, seem to have worn quite simple garments. We know, from an illuminated manuscript preserved in the library of Corpus Christi College, Cambridge, that King Athelstan wore a short yellow tunic with a narrow gold border, a blue cloak and red hose; and we know from an illuminated grant of lands to the Abbey of Winchester (AD 966) that King Edgar was similarly clad, except that his tunic was shorter and his legs enclosed in narrow bands like puttees.

We have considerable information, again from illuminated manuscripts, about the dress of Anglo-Saxon women. The principal garments were the tunic or kirtle, worn over a smock

53

and put on over the head; the super-tunic or roc, also put on over the head and sometimes hitched up over the girdle to show the garment beneath (it had embroidered borders at neck, hem and sleeves); and the mantle, sometimes as long as the tunic and fastened under the chin. The hair was concealed by a veil or 'head-rail', long enough to be crossed over the bosom and hang down to the knees.

The coming of the Danes made very little difference to costume in England, except that the Danish men wore their hair longer and were much given to the wearing of bracelets, which were regarded as marks of military prowess. The Norman Conquest, however, was quite a different matter, for the descendants of the Norsemen who had established themselves in Normandy were, by this time, completely Frenchified, having even abandoned the language of their forefathers. Edward the Confessor, who ascended the throne in 1042, was himself half Norman, and even Harold, who succeeded him, had spent long periods in France. The monkish chroniclers of the time were already complaining that the English had forgotten their usual simplicity, had trimmed their hair, shortened their tunics and generally adopted French modes.

Nevertheless, there was sufficient difference for the English spies who were sent out before the Battle of Hastings to report that the invading army consisted of nothing but priests, that is, men with short hair, the back of the neck being shaved. It was to celebrate this battle that Queen Matilda and her ladies embroidered the long strip of linen, wrongly called a tapestry, which is still preserved at Bayeux and which serves as an admirable illustration of the costume of the period. We see King *Ill. 46* Edward in his long tunic receiving messengers in tunics shorter than knee-length, and over them the super-tunic, which was a loose, circular garment put on over the head. Stockings had ornamented tops, visible below the tunic and allowed to wrinkle so that they look very much like the leg-bandages already described. Leg-bandages were also worn, bound either spirally or criss-cross over the stockings.

54

46 King Edward the Confessor, from the Bayeux tapestry. Late eleventh century

47 Scene from a play by Terence, derived from a Carolingian manuscript. This bears witness to the comparatively static forms of costume over several centuries

Scholars have long been aware of the influence of the Crusades in modifying the costume of Western Europe. It is true that already before the eleventh century there was contact with the Mohammedan world through Sicily and Spain, and the rich stuffs of the Orient had thus found their way to the West, but only in very small quantities and out of reach of all but wealthy kings. When the Normans captured Sicily in 1060, they found a civilization vastly superior to their own in learning and crafts-manship, and a degree of luxury unknown to them before. Many of the craftsmen remained under their new rulers and were eagerly employed by them in weaving and goldsmiths' work. This patronage continued when Frederick of Hohen-staufen, crowned as Holy Roman Emperor in 1220, established his Court at Palermo. Under his tolerant rule all the arts flourished and he was himself, in his tastes and his garments, more like an Oriental sultan than a Christian king.

In Spain the gradual conquest of the lands occupied by the Moors resulted in the capture of rich booty: jewellery and fine tissues far more luxurious than the contemporary products of Christian Europe. Then came the Crusades and the reopening of trade with the Near East. But the returning Crusaders brought back with them not only Oriental materials but the clothes themselves, or a knowledge of their cut. Western ladies adopted the Mohammedan veil, or a least a wimple concealing the lower part of the face. On the other hand, they began to mould their gowns to the figure by means of buttons down the side, the upper part of the gown being thus drawn tight over the bust. The sleeves became immensely long and very wide at the wrist, as can be seen in one of the most valuable docu-ments of the period, the *Hortus Deliciarum* of the Abbess of Landsberg in Alsace, which was produced in about 1175. Another valuable source of information is to be found in the sculptures of the cathedrals which began to be erected in France and Germany in the twelfth century.

Ills. 49–51

Part of the confusion in descriptions of medieval costume is due to the failure to distinguish between hose and breeches.

48 Crusader doing homage, thirteenth century

Even such established historians of costume as Hottenroth, Viollet-le-Duc and Racinet have failed to do this, and it was not until quite recent years that the distinction was made plain by writers like Dorothy Hartley and C. Willett Cunnington.

In the eleventh century breeches or *braies* were ankle-length trousers kept in place by a cord threaded through the top, rather low over the hips. The nobility wore them fitted to the leg, the lower classes loose and rather baggy. They were sometimes worn with leg-bandages bound spirally or in a criss-cross pattern. Hose, or *chausses* (i.e. stockings), were cut to the shape of the leg out of wool or linen cloth, knitting being practically unknown in England until the reign of Elizabeth I. In the eleventh century they reached to just below the knee, with a patterned top, rather like that of modern golfing stockings. But in the twelfth century they rose to mid-thigh, being made wide enough at the top to be pulled over the *braies*. Some ended at the ankles, some had a strip like a stirrup under the instep and some were provided with a thin leather sole obviating the use of shoes indoors. They were sometimes striped and brightly coloured. Meanwhile, the breeches were shrinking to become invisible drawers. With labourers at work they became a mere breech-clout.

49 Shepherds, from Chartres Cathedral, *c.* 1150. They wear the short tunics of the common people and leg-coverings made of narrow bands of material

50 A sainted king and queen, from Chartres Cathedral, *c.* 1150. The long, open sleeves should be noted

51 The Lady Uta, one of the founder-figures in Naumburg Cathedral, *c.* 1245

52 Scene showing peasant costume, c. 1335-40

The twelfth century showed little essential modification, except that the tunic was more closely fitting and sleeves showed a sudden widening at the wrist. The hood, which originally had formed part of the cloak, became a separate garment in the second half of the century, with a small shoulder-length cape attached to it. There were several forms of hat, ranging from *Ill. 52* the pointed 'Phrygian' cap to something resembling a beret, and to hats with wide brims which were worn over the hood when travelling. Indoors, men sometimes wore the coif of plain linen covering the ears and tied under the chin.

In female dress a new style appeared about 1130, the bodice of the gown, at least for the upper classes, being moulded so as to fit tightly down to the hips, the skirt below that being cut wide and falling in folds to the feet. It was sometimes sufficiently *Ill. 53* long to form a train. The super-tunic also was more closely fitting and with wider sleeves. The veil was sometimes kept in place by a half-circle or complete circle of gold worn round the forehead. In addition, from the late twelfth century to the early fourteenth century, the barbette was worn. This was a

60

53 The elaborate clothes of a knight and his lady, c. 1335–40

54, 55, 56 Brass-rubbings from sepulchral monuments, dated 1375, 1391 and 1430

linen band passing under the chin and drawn up over the temples. Worn during the same period was the wimple or gorget. It was made of fine white linen or silk, covered the neck and part of the bosom, and was sometimes tucked into the top of the gown, the ends being then drawn up and pinned to the top of the head under the veil to frame the face.

It was in the second half of the fourteenth century that clothes both for men and for women took on new forms, and something emerges which we can already call 'fashion'. The old *gipon*, which was beginning to be called a 'doublet', was padded in the front to swell out the chest and was worn much shorter, so short indeed that the moralists of the period

62

57, 58, 59 Rubbings dated 1437, *c.* 1480 and *c.* 1501. The ladies' headdresses show a growing elaboration in the late fourteenth and fifteenth centuries

denounced it as indecent. It was worn very tight, with buttons down the front and with a belt low over the hips.

The upper classes wore over the *gipon* a garment known as a *cote-hardie*. This was the super-tunic of a previous age, but it was now low-necked and tight-fitting and buttoned down the front. The *cote-hardie* of the lower classes was looser and, having no buttons, was put on over the head. The length of the fashionable *cote-hardie* gradually diminished and the edge was often dagged – that is, cut in curious patterns. The sleeves were tight to the elbow but then flared out, becoming wide enough to hang down to the knees or even lower. About 1375 the *cote-hardie* began to have a collar.

Ill. 54

63

A characteristic garment from about 1380 to 1450 was the *houppelande*, later to be known as the 'gown'. It fitted the shoulders and was loose below, with a belt at the waist. Its length varied, being longest for ceremonial occasions. The sleeves were extremely wide and sometimes so long as to reach to the ground. It had a high upright collar, sometimes reaching to the ears, and its edge was dagged into fantastic shapes. Chaucer, in *The Parson's Tale*, blames 'so much pouncing of chisel to make holes, so much dagging of shears, with the superfluity in length of the aforesaid gowns, trailing in the dung and in the mire, on horse and eke on foot, as well of man as of woman'.

Women, in general, were less extravagantly clad than men, so far as the shape of their garments was concerned. The main item of their dress was the kirtle or gown, close-fitting down to the waist and then flaring out in a full skirt hanging in folds. The sleeves were so tight-fitting that they had to be buttoned over the lower area and were sufficiently long to extend over half the hand. Over the gown was worn the *cote-hardie*, similar to that worn by men. The sleeves had long streamers or tippets

Ill. 60 which sometimes trailed on the ground. From the middle of the fourteenth century it was fashionable to wear the sideless sur-coat, a curious garment with large openings at the sides. The front formed a kind of stiffened stomacher known as a 'plackard'.

The effect was of tight lacing – one of the most potent weapons of fashion through the ages – which now, for the first time, began to be exploited. Another innovation, with an even greater erotic appeal, was décolletage, the cutting away of the top of the robe to reveal part of the bosom. Yet another was the abandonment of the veil, which henceforward was worn only by nuns and widows. Instead there began a long series of headdresses, growing ever more elaborate and fantastic until the end of the fifteenth century.

We can watch this development in tomb sculptures, and in
Ills. 54–9 particular in the memorial tablet known as a 'brass'. This was a sheet of brass cut out in the shape of a figure and engraved with

60 *The Marriage of Giovanni (?) Arnolfini and Giovanna Cenami(?)*, by Jan van Eyck, 1434

details of the costume of the deceased, and let in to the pavement of a church. Curiously enough such memorials are to be found only in England and in certain parts of Flanders. They are a most valuable source of documentation, since it is easy to take rubbings from them, and such rubbings might almost be called the fashion plates of the later Middle Ages. Above all, they have the inestimable advantage of being dated.

Already, towards the end of the thirteenth century, the crespine had made its appearance, worn with the barbette and the fillet. This was a kind of hairnet, and was a somewhat startling innovation, since previous ages had considered visible female hair to be immoral. The next stage was to wear the crespine by itself, the alternative being vertical plaits on each side of the face. These are very characteristic of the last quarter of the fourteenth century. At the same period the veil re-appeared, but in a new form. This was the goffered veil or 'nebula' headdress, made of a half-circle of linen framing the face. Sometimes it was composed of several layers and resembled the ruff of the second half of the sixteenth century, except that, of course, it was worn not round the neck but round the face. The fillet also took on a new shape, forming two hollow ornamental pillars through which the hair was drawn. The effect, in contrast to that of the rounded 'nebula' headdress, was extremely square, the face being, as it were, enclosed in a frame.

Towards the end of the fourteenth century appeared also the 'cushion' headdress, which was a kind of padded roll worn over a hairnet. The hair was coiled above each ear in small knobs known as 'templers'. For the first third of the fifteenth century the effect was one of breadth. Sometimes this was pushed to an extreme, the width of the two templers combined being twice that of the face.

Ill. 68

The horned headdress which came in about 1410 had a wire structure like the horns of a cow on which was draped the veil. This was followed by the heart-shaped headdress, the name itself being a sufficient description. Both of these styles were

61, 62 Engravings by Israel van Meckenem showing Italian fashion *c*. 1470 (left) and North European *c*. 1485 (right). Note particularly the difference in female headdress and male shoe

attempts to use the veil as a decorative attraction, the opposite of its original purpose. To this extent the denunciations of contemporary moralists may seem justified.

The second half of the century saw a number of new varieties. Instead of being broad, headdresses tended to be high, sometimes extremely so. The sausage-shaped roll of padded material forming a narrow U over the forehead, known in a primitive form to the previous generation, was now much elongated and tilted backward. The same happened to the 'turban' headdress and the 'chimney-pot' headdress. (These are not contemporary names but attempts by modern scholars at descriptive labels.) The latter had a veil attached to the top.

The *hennin* or 'steeple' headdress was much worn in France. In England it took the shape of a truncated cone and was therefore not very different from the 'chimney-pot' headdress. A

67

better name, perhaps, would be 'flower-pot'. Most spectacular
of all was the 'butterfly' headdress. This was a wire structure
attached to a small cap or caul in which the hair was enclosed.
It rose high above the head and supported a diaphanous veil
in the shape of a butterfly's wings. It was a very popular
fashion up to about 1485.

Men's clothes in the second half of the fifteenth century
showed a number of developments. The main garment was
still the doublet, but it could be worn extremely short, so short
as to demand the use of a codpiece at times. It began to develop

63 *Wedding of Boccaccio Adimari*. Florentine, *c.* 1470. Probably from a *cassone* or dower-chest. The liripipe hood has developed into a hat (above right), now part of official dress

a high stand-up collar. The *cote-hardie* was replaced by the jacket or jerkin, increasingly tight-fitting, and the shoulders were padded to increase the apparent width of the body. The sleeves were generally full and sometimes detachable.

The *houppelande* was now called the 'gown' and was worn by older men, doctors, magistrates and the like. It fell in vertical

pleats to the ankles and was fastened down the front with hooks and eyes. It was worn with or without a belt, and the sleeves were usually very full. When they hung low down they were known as 'surplice sleeves'. It was usual to line the gown, sometimes with fur.

There was considerable variety in male headgear. Until about 1380 the hood with long liripipe had been almost universally worn. Then someone had the bright idea of sticking his *head* into the opening where his face should have been, winding the hood, with its dagged edge, round the head in the form of a turban and tying it in place with the liripipe. Philip the Good is shown wearing a headdress of this type.

Ills. 63, 67

A development from this was the *chaperon*, which consisted of a circular padded roll to which was attached a gorget consisting of folds of material cut in decorative shapes. The effect was rather similar to that of the turban already described, but it was, so to speak, 'ready-made', required no arranging and

64 *Duchess of Urbino*, by Piero della Francesca (after 1473)

65 *Portrait of a lady in red.* Florentine, *c.* 1470.

66 *Margaret of Denmark, Queen of Scotland*, ascribed to Hugo van der Goes, 1476

It is thought that the eyebrows and hair on the forehead were shaved in imitation of classical sculpture

could be put on and off without difficulty. It had a strange history. It was sometimes worn on the shoulder instead of the head, and in this position shrank and became a badge of livery. In its final term it became the cockade on the nineteenth-century coachman's hat.

During the fifteenth century hats were increasingly worn, and assumed many different shapes. Some had flat crowns and narrow brims, some were very tall and had no brims. Crowns tapered or ballooned out. Something resembling the Turkish fez (and frequently red in colour) can be seen in contemporary paintings. Some hats were not unlike the modern bowler, some were adorned with plumes. Towards the end of the century a flat cap was worn, with a turned-up brim adorned with a single jewelled ornament.

Until the 1480s men's shoes were markedly pointed, sometimes fantastically so. This tendency had been seen as early as 1360 and was regarded with disfavour by the ecclesiastical and

71

civil authorities. King Edward III even enacted a sumptuary law which laid down that 'no Knight under the estate of a lord, esquire or gentleman, nor any other person, shall wear any shoes or boots having spikes or points exceeding the length of two inches, under the forfeiture of forty pence'. This, like all sumptuary laws, was completely ineffective, for in the following reign, the 'spikes or points' sometimes reached the length of eighteen inches or more. Such shoes were known as *crackowes*, or *poulaines*, the terms being corruptions, respectively, of Cracow and Poland. Poland was then part of the Kingdom of Bohemia, and the names are explained by the fact that King Richard II married Anne of Bohemia and the gentlemen who came in her suite to England wore shoes with extremely pointed toes. The extreme fashion lasted until about 1410, and pointed shoes of some kind until the advent of the Tudors. The revolution in fashion this implied is dealt with in the next chapter.

67 Philip the Good, Duke of Burgundy, receiving a copy of the *Chroniques de Hainaut*. Flemish, 1448

68 Christine de Pisan presenting
her book of poems to Isabel of
Bavaria, Queen of France. French,
early fifteenth century. The ladies'
headdresses are of two kinds:
à cornes, and with the veil raised
from the face by means of pins

69 Extreme form of the *poulaine* or
crackowe, from the *Chronique
d'Angleterre*. Flemish, fifteenth
century

CHAPTER FOUR

The Renaissance and the sixteenth century

THE FASHIONS, and art forms generally, of the Gothic North had never been fully accepted in Italy, and by the middle of the fifteenth century Italian modes had already diverged considerably from those of the rest of medieval Europe. In their style of headdress, for example, the fine ladies painted by Van *Ill. 70* der Weyden in the Netherlands and those painted in Italy by *Ill. 71* Ghirlandaio were very different. Elaborate *bourrelets* (stuffed and padded hair-styles) were draped with veils in the North, whereas hair-styles were much more natural and less formal in Italy; yet the fashion for plucking the hairline to give a high forehead was universal. Different too was the cut of the sleeves, close-fitting in the North, swelling out in Italy, with slashes through which the white chemise could be seen. Often the sleeves were made detachable, and were heavily decorated – a reflection of the enormous increase in luxury brought about by the mercantile prosperity of the Italian cities.

The invasion of Italy by the French King Charles VIII doubtless introduced the Italians to French fashions, but in general the influence was the other way. The Renaissance was, so to speak, transplanted over the Alps, and if Charles VIII was *Ill. 80* still a medieval king, Francis I was a Renaissance monarch.

So, in England, was Henry VIII. It is true that the reign of his father, Henry VII, had already seen many modifications in medieval costume. The line, instead of being vertical, was now horizontal; the shoes, instead of being excessively pointed, became broad-toed, as if to echo the new style of architecture with its flattened arch. Ladies' headdresses ceased to be replicas of Gothic pinnacles and began to resemble Tudor windows. And with the advent of the new century a curious Germanism

74

70 *Portrait of a lady*, by Rogier van der Weyden, *c.* 1455

71 *Giovanna Tornabuoni*, by Domenico Ghirlandaio, 1488

72 *Nuremberg housewife and Venetian lady*. Drawing by Dürer, 1495.

These show the variation in hairdressing and clothes between northern Europe and Italy. Italian influence is evident in the very fine veil and black necklace of Rogier van der Weyden's northern lady

73 Jacob Fugger 'the Rich', the Emperor's banker, with Matthäus Schwarz, his chief accountant, 1519

74 German *Landsknecht*, *c.* 1530. An example in their extreme form of the slashings worn by the German mercenaries but influencing male costume all over Europe

76

began to influence the dress of the fashionable in both France and England.

Much has been written about this strange development, but contemporary chroniclers are almost unanimous in ascribing it to the victory of the Swiss over Charles the Bold, Duke of

Burgundy, at the Battle of Grandson (1476). Much plunder of silk and other costly materials fell to the victors, who slashed the booty to pieces and used it to patch their own ragged clothes. The Swiss troops were copied by the German mercenaries, and from them the fashion spread to the French Court, probably introduced by the Guise family, itself half German. The marriage of Henry VII's sister Mary to Louis XII of France caused the English to adopt the *landsknecht* fashion also.

Ill. 76 Slashing indeed (i.e. the practice of cutting slits in the material of garments and pulling the lining through) became almost universal in the early 1500s; but it was in Germany that it reached its most extravagant extreme. For not only the doublet but the breeches were slashed; indeed, quite literally, 'cut to ribbons'. Nether garments consisted of broad bands of material falling to the knees and sometimes to the ankles. Care was taken that the bands on each leg should form different patterns, and they could even be of different colours. We hear in the chronicles of 'hose made in the German manner, the

76, 77 *Duke Henry of Saxony and his wife*, by Lucas Cranach, 1514. The slashing in men's clothes was matched by the rich decoration of women's garments

78, 79 Two stages in the development of the ruff: left, *Katherina Knoblau-chin*, by Conrad Faber, 1532. Right, *Portrait of an unknown man*, by Bartolommeo Veneto, before 1540

one [leg] yellow, the other black, slashed with sixteen ells of taffeta'.

Slashing spread to women's clothes, but was never as prevalent. This extravagant fashion was more suitable for breeches than for large areas of fabric such as skirts. Indeed, female dress at this period is much more modest than male costume. Skirts, however, were ampler and more richly *Ill. 77* embroidered than in earlier reigns. Over the kirtle, which consisted of a skirt and bodice sewn together, was worn the gown, falling in ample folds to the ground from a tight-fitting waist. The sleeves ceased to be tight and became very large indeed, with a deep turn-back of fur, as can be seen in Holbein's portraits. There was much use of fur both by men and by women: lynx, wolf and sable being the favourites. The neck was cut square and low, and above it could be seen the top of the *Ills. 81–2* chemise. Men also, in the early years of the century, were

80 *Francis I of France*. Attributed to François Clouet. Early sixteenth century

81, 82 *Helen of Bavaria*, by Hans Schöpfer, *c.* 1563–6, and *Jane Seymour*, *c.* 1536–7, by Holbein. These two illustrations show the square décolletage and the contrast between the German and English modes of headgear

décolleté, with the top of the shirt showing. Through this was threaded a string, and when this was drawn tight we can already see the beginnings of what was to be the ruff of the second half of the century. *Ills. 79, 80*

The main male garment was the doublet, sometimes long enough to fall to the knee. It had an opening in the front through which could be seen the codpiece. The sleeves grew gradually wider and were often paned or slashed. Sometimes double sleeves were worn, one pair hanging loose and of a different colour. The materials most in favour were velvet, satin and cloth-of-gold. We know from his Wardrobe Account that Henry VIII possessed a doublet of purple satin, embroidered with gold and silver thread and sewn all over with pearls. Over the doublet was worn the jacket or jerkin, either double *Ill. 83*

83 *Henry VIII.* School of Holbein. The acme of masculinity in dress with wide shoulders and a codpiece

breasted or closed down the front with laces or buttons; over this was the gown, fitting loosely over the shoulders, falling in ample folds to the feet and usually edged with fur.

The nether garments consisted of breeches and stockings sewn together. The top edge was secured to the doublet by means of points, i.e. laces threaded through eyelet holes in both garments and tied in small bows. These points were made of linen or silk thread lipped with metal tags, known as 'aiglets'. The shoes were at first extremely broad, in the shape called

82

'duck-bill'. The heels were flat, the soles of leather or cork, *Ill. 83* the uppers of leather, velvet or silk. Shoes were often slashed and adorned with jewels.

Hats were worn indoors as well as out, and for the most part took the form of a soft, low bonnet. Sometimes this had a brim which could be turned up in front and kept in place by a jewel; or the brim could be cut away in the front, but with side pieces which could be turned down over the ears. The brim was sometimes slashed in various patterns. A wide-brimmed hat was worn by travellers and country folk. A curious survival from the medieval period was the linen coif tied under the chin. In the sixteenth century its use was confined to the elderly or to lawyers and other professional men. Men wore their hair long, and under Henry VII and in the early years of Henry VIII's reign had clean-shaven faces. But in 1535, according to Stow's *Annals*, 'The King commanded all about his Court to poll

84 Costume plate by Jost Amman showing German bourgeois dress, *c.* 1560

their heads, and to give them example, he caused his own head to be polled, and from henceforth his beard to be . . . no more shaven.' It is thought that, in this, he was following the fashion inaugurated by the French King Francis I.

Some of the greatest portraits of all time were painted in the sixteenth century: one has only to mention the names of Holbein, Bronzino, Titian. But for the most part these artists painted very grand people in their very grandest clothes. For the physical appearance of the less exalted we must turn to German *Kleinmeister* such as Aldegrever, the Beham brothers,

Ill. 84

85 Opposite, *The Ambassadors*, by Holbein, 1533

86 *Thomas Cranmer*, by Gerhardt Flicke, 1546

Jost Amman and Virgil Solis. The Behams show us the peasants, Aldegrever the patricians, while Jost Amman plunges us right into the everyday life of the middle classes.

Naturally, these peasant and middle-class garments exhibited none of the extravagance of those worn in Court circles. But every prosperous citizen possessed what the Germans called a *Schaube*, an overcoat shaped like a cassock but generally without sleeves. If it had sleeves, they hung empty behind the visible sleeves of the garment worn underneath. The *Schaube*, often lined with fur, became the typical garment of the scholar. Luther wore one and thereby dictated the costume of the Lutheran clergy to the present day. In England Thomas Cranmer wore a similar garment, and this, with the chain round the neck, became the ancestor of the accepted costume of mayors. The vestigial sleeves of the sleeved variety can still be seen in academic dress.

Ill. 86

The clothes of the upper classes during the first half of the sixteenth century were extremely brightly coloured. We learn from the wardrobe inventories of Henry VIII that he possessed, among many others, doublets of blue and red velvet lined with cloth-of-gold. In 1535 Thomas Cromwell made his royal master a present of a purple velvet doublet embroidered in gold; and some of the King's garments were so heavily encrusted with diamonds, rubies and pearls that the underlying material was invisible.

Red was a favourite colour. In the well-known portrait of the Earl of Surrey, formerly attributed to Holbein, the young nobleman is shown completely clad in various shades of scarlet. In Cranach's portraits of German princes nearly all of them are wearing red, and, in spite of sumptuary laws, the middle classes imitated them as far as they dared. It is a curious comment on human aspiration that during the Peasants' Revolt in Germany, one of the demands of the insurgents was that they should be allowed to wear red clothes like their betters.

87 *Emperor Charles V with his dog*, by Titian, 1532

88 *Anne of Austria, Queen of Spain*, by Sanchez Coello, 1571. A further step in the development of the ruff

89 *A tailor*, by Giovanni Battista Moroni, *c.* 1571, an example of middle-class costume

90 *Portrait of a young man*, by Angelo Bronzino, *c.* 1540. The clothes of the upper classes show strong Spanish influence (*see also Ill. 91*)

And then, about the middle of the century, everything changed. The German domination of European fashion, with its bright colours and fantastic forms, gave way to Spanish modes, tight-fitting and sombre, preferably black. This was partly due to the personal taste of the Emperor Charles V, who was famous for the sobriety of his dress, and partly to the growing power of Spain. When in 1556 Philip II succeeded Charles V as King of Spain, the Spanish Court became the admired exemplar for all Europe. Even the French King Henry II followed the Spanish fashion and almost always wore black.

Ill. 87

In England the tendency to wear more sombre colours can already be seen in the closing years of the reign of Henry VIII. The boy King Edward VI, who succeeded him, was unlikely to have much influence on fashion, and when he died and Mary Tudor ascended the throne, the trend was emphasized. Her

91 *Pierre Quthe*, by François Clouet, 1562

marriage in 1554 to the Spanish King completed the revolution, for although the clothes of the Spanish courtiers who came to England in his train at first seemed strange to English eyes, the English soon adopted similar garments themselves. Even when Mary was succeeded by Elizabeth, even when England and Spain were at war, the Spanish influence persisted, and can be noted, with little modification, until the end of the century.

Ill. 93

It was not only in colour, or the lack of it, that the new fashions differed from those of the preceding generation. There was a real difference in cut. Cunnington sums up the special features of the new mode as 'bombast, small waists and the introduction of knitting' (*Handbook of English Costume in the Sixteenth Century*). Bombast was the stuffing used in doublets and hose in order to swell them out, eliminating all folds and creases. It consisted of rags, flock, horsehair, cotton or even bran, although this last sometimes led to disaster, since all the bran ran out if the clothes got torn. The bombasting of the doublet over the chest and the stuffing out of breeches naturally made the waist seem smaller, and the effect was increased by the use of tight-lacing. The short, bombasted breeches, especially in the form of trunk hose, exposed a considerable expanse of leg, and the introduction of knitting made it possible for leg coverings to fit the limbs more neatly than they had done before.

The effect of all this was a new rigidity and *hauteur*, reflecting the stiff and proud etiquette of the Spanish Court. Gone were the easy flowing lines of the costume of the earlier part of the century, when clothes seemed to express a man's own personality, even his own fantasy. Instead men now seemed to be indicating their membership of an aristocratic caste. They hold themselves upright in padded and stiffened garments which form a veritable *cuirasse*. Art historians have noticed that Court portrait painting all over Europe represents its subjects standing, with one foot advanced, in an attitude of proud withdrawal, hieratic and stiff. And this effect was enhanced by the growth of the ruff.

92 *Mary I, Queen of England*, by Antonis Mor, 1554
93 *Queen Elizabeth I 'Rainbow Portrait'*, c. 1600

We have already noted the draw-string through the upper edge of the shirt from which the ruff derived. It was only necessary to draw the string tight round the neck and an incipient ruff was already in being. When, as in the 1570s, it appeared above the high-standing collar of the doublet, it held the head high in an attitude of disdain. It goes without saying *Ills. 94–5* that the ruff was a mark of aristocratic privilege. It is an extreme example of the tendency of men's clothes to show that their wearers do not need to work, or indeed to engage in any strenuous pursuit; and, as the century progressed, ruffs grew larger and larger until it is difficult to see how their wearers could have conveyed food to their mouths.

The ruff is an example of the 'hierarchical' element in dress. Women wore it too, but in female dress there is always another element to be noted. This – the 'Seduction Principle' as it has been called – is an attempt to exploit the wearer's charms as a

91

94 *Magdalena, Duchess of Neuburg*, portrait formerly attributed to Peter Candid (de Witte), *c.* 1613. The elaborate triple ruff of the early seventeenth century

95 *Queen Elizabeth at Blackfriars*, by Marcus Gheeraerts, *c.* 1600

woman, as, for example, by the use of décolletage. Women
wished to wear a ruff in order to show their status in society:
they also wished to be attractive as women. The 'Elizabethan
compromise' was to open the ruff in front so as to expose the
bosom, and to allow it to rise in gauze wings at the back of the
head. This can be seen quite clearly in contemporary portraits of
Queen Elizabeth.

Ills. 93, 95

The effect of the vertical line now dominant in costume was accentuated by the abandonment of flat caps (although apprentices were still compelled by law to wear them by an Act of Parliament of 1571) in favour of hats of various kinds. Some of the hats were in fact bonnets with a tall crown, which was sometimes stiffened with buckram; others were true hats made of stiff or stiffened materials. One of these was the so-called *copotain* which had a high conical crown; another variety resembled a modern bowler. They could be made of beaver, felt or leather, and could, if wished, be furnished with a plume and a jewel attached to the hat-band. There were also hats with broad brims and flat crowns, affected by magistrates and professional men. These were worn flat on the head: the Elizabethan gallant nearly always wore his hat at an angle or on the back of the head.

Ill. 98

Women, too, began to wear hats in place of the hoods or bonnets with which they had been content for so long. At first

they were used chiefly for riding or travelling. They were similar to men's hats but smaller and were often worn over a linen cap. But, as hairdressing became more elaborate, this coif was gradually discarded. The headdress usually hid the back hair, which was plaited behind the head, but the front hair was visible, and considerable variation in arrangement can be seen in contemporary portraits. Until the 1570s it was often fluffed out at the temples with a central parting. Then it was turned back over a pad, and finally raised over a wire support known as a 'palisadoe'. Queen Elizabeth set the fashion for dyeing the hair red, and many women, like herself, must have found it necessary to make use of false hair. In her old age the Queen wore a wig.

The rigidity which marked men's clothes in the second half of the sixteenth century was even more pronounced in those of women. The stomacher which formed the front of the bodice was stiffened with buckram or pasteboard and held in

96, 97 Opposite, three granddaughters and the son of Mildred, Lady Burghley, from her tomb in Westminster Abbey, 1589. The little girls' hair is enclosed in a kind of chignon. The advantage of sculpture is that it enables us to see the ruff from the back

98 Middle-class and servant's costume from *Description of England*, late sixteenth century

99 *Rubens and his wife Isabella Brant*, by Rubens, 1610. The painter wears the new falling collar, his wife the ruff. Her corsage is kept in place by a rigid busk

100 *Sigmund Feierabendt, the bibliophile*, by J. Sadeler, 1587. Costume of the middle-class scholar

place by busks, often of wood and therefore unbending. The skirt was swelled out by means of the farthingale. Its origin was universally acknowledged. It was the 'Spanish farthingale' or 'vertingale', and in its original form it consisted of an underskirt distended by hoops of wire, wood or whalebone, growing larger towards the bottom of the skirt. It therefore very closely resembled the nineteenth-century crinoline in its construction. It first appeared in England about the year 1545 and was soon worn by all women but those of the labouring classes.

The 'French farthingale', which came in about 1580, was more of a Court garment. It was called the 'wheel farthingale', which is a sufficient description of its general effect. It was as if the wearer were standing inside a wheel, with the skirt attached to the outer rim and falling vertically to the ground. In the well-known painting *Queen Elizabeth at Blackfriars*, the *Ill. 95* Queen and all her ladies are seen wearing this singularly unbecoming garment, which made women look as if they were hobby-horses. Rather similar was the 'Italian farthingale', made

97

101 Ball at the Court of King Henry III of France, late sixteenth century

of wire or whalebone and worn slightly tilted at the back by means of a cushion, like a primitive bustle. The width could be as much as forty-eight inches.

A more popular fashion, outside Court circles, was the 'roll farthingale', vulgarly known as the 'bum roll'. This consisted of a padded roll of cloth in the shape of a polony, or boiling sausage, the two ends being joined together at the front of the body with tapes. By the end of the century it had become unfashionable, as is indicated by a character in Ben Jonson's *The Poetaster* who remarks that she has 'debased' herself from the farthingale to 'those bum rolls'.

In addition to the boned bodice and farthingale-extended skirt, women's principal garment at this period was the gown, which fell in folds from fitted shoulders, leaving a gap in the front through which the dress underneath could be seen. The sleeves were puffed, and ended above the elbow to reveal the

102 *Sir Christopher Hatton*, Anon., 1.   103 *Sir Walter Raleigh*, Anon., c. 1588

undersleeve. Sometimes long, vestigial, hanging sleeves were worn, attached to the upper sleeve. Other garments mentioned in contemporary inventories were the coat, a kind of loose jacket worn for warmth; the frock, which seems to have been a loose gown; and the cassock, which was of a similar form but with loose, open sleeves. For travelling, cloaks were worn and also a garment known as a 'safeguard', which seems to have been an over-skirt of plain material used both for warmth and to protect the rich stuff of the gown.

Men, too, began to employ a greater variety of garments. *Ills. 102–3* The doublet was still the main item in a gentleman's wardrobe, but over this could be worn the jerkin or jacket, often sleeveless. The cloak had now become indispensable, but it was no longer the long cloak of the preceding generation but a short cloak, sometimes hung from one shoulder. Although it had originally been a riding cloak, it was worn, during the second half of the

99

sixteenth century, indoors as well as out. It was made of rich materials, and the really fashionable man required three cloaks, one for morning, one for afternoon and one for evening. Cloaks sometimes had standing collars, and were sometimes provided with a tippet, usually of velvet.

Men also wore the garment known as a 'cassock', which was a loose jacket reaching to the hips, and a gabardine which was a long, loose overcoat with wide sleeves. But the most curious item in the Elizabethan gentleman's wardrobe was the mandilion or mandeville. We cannot do better than quote Cunnington's description: 'Originally a military habit, it was a loose hip-length jacket with standing collar and hanging "coat" sleeves (later sham) and wings. The side seams were open, producing a front and back panel. It was buttoned from collar to chest only, and put on over the head. It was frequently worn "Collie-Westonward", or awry, "Collie Weston" being a Cheshire saying for anything that goes wrong. The garment *Ill. 103* was thus worn sideways, with the front and back panels draping the shoulders, while one sleeve hung down in front and the other behind' (*Handbook of English Costume in the Sixteenth Century*).

Male nether garments showed some peculiar variations in the second half of the century. Ordinary trunk hose could now *Ill. 95* be worn with 'canions'. These were breeches worn underneath the trunk hose (and often of a different material) and reaching to the knee. The stockings could be drawn over them, so that we might say that the 'hose' of the medieval period has now divided into three separate garments.

True breeches, if we may call them such, dispensed with trunk hose altogether. They could take various forms. 'Venetians' were rather baggy breeches fastening below the knee with buttons or points. They came in about 1570, but were most popular in the last twenty years of the century. When very baggy they were called 'galligaskins', 'gascoynes' or 'slops'.

With such garments stockings acquired a new importance. They were cut on the cross from cloth until about 1590, after

100

104 *Richard Sackville, Earl of Dorset*, by Isaac Oliver, 1616. He wears the transitional form between the ruff and the falling collar

which they were increasingly replaced by knitted stockings, sometimes of silk. They were sometimes of bright colours, yellow being a favourite, and were often adorned with clocks *Ill. 104* of coloured silk or even with gold thread, and were gartered in various ways: by a simple ribbon (which could, however, be adorned with gold thread or even with jewels) tied below *Ill. 95* the knee, the bow being at the side; or by cross-gartering, which did not in the least resemble what many Shakespearean producers imagine it to have been, i.e. a kind of trellis-work covering the entire leg. Cross-gartering, which was fashionable from 1560 onwards, was formed by a piece of ribbon encircling the leg below the knee, crossed at the back, brought forward above the knee and tied in a bow.

Footwear consisted of shoes or boots. The shoes were *Ill. 104* moderately rounded and were just beginning, as the century closed, to have heels. They could be made of leather, silk, velvet or plain cloth. The soles could be of leather or cork. Pumps and slippers were worn indoors. Boots, which until the last quarter of the century were used only for riding, became general wear, even indoors. The fashionable variety was close-fitting and reached to the thigh, the top being sometimes turned down in different ways. Such boots were only made possible by the improvements in leather-dressing originating in Cordoba. Our English word 'cordwainer' means a man who has derived his craft from this Spanish city.

Spain was also responsible for the fine leather gloves so much prized by the Elizabethans and which only began to be manufactured in England from about 1580. The most usual form was provided with gauntlets, which were often decorated with gold thread and fringed. They could also be perfumed, and were in general carried in the hand or tucked into the belt. The elegant gentleman also required a handkerchief, which was made of fine linen, embroidered or edged with lace. The clothes and accessories of the upper classes in Europe had indeed reached an astonishing degree of elaboration and refinement by the end of the sixteenth century.

CHAPTER FIVE

The seventeenth century

WE HAVE SEEN that during the second half of the sixteenth century Spain set the dominant tone in fashion. This influence persisted into the 1600s, but with certain modifications, notably in the abandonment of the stuffed and busked 'peascod' doublets and in the widening of the sleeves. The ruffs, too, became smaller in France and England, but continued to grow even larger in the Netherlands.

The doublet in the early years of the century had a short skirt consisting of a number of overlapping tabs, but from about 1610 these tabs were longer and curved down in front to a sharp point. The garment was provided with a high-standing collar buttoning in front, but generally concealed by the ruff. This was carried over from the preceding century but with certain variations, being sometimes in double or treble layers of tubular pleats starched by means of 'setting sticks'. Ruffs were usually white but sometimes yellow. The invention of starch, denounced by Puritan moralists as a new vanity, at least allowed the ruff to dispense with the wire frame or 'underpropper' which had previously been necessary.

In France, Henry IV, in contrast to Henry III, was a man of simple tastes. He was by no means a prude, being famous as *le Vert Galant* for his amours; but he had no liking for extravagance in dress, and issued several sumptuary laws, largely aimed at preventing the import of expensive materials of foreign manufacture. This had most effect on the dress of the *bourgeoisie*, members of which began to wear clothes made of wool. The courtiers continued to wear silk, but with fewer trimmings of gold and silver thread.

105–8 French noblemen and noblewoman, by Abraham Bosse, c. 1629–36. All the men have the characteristic 'bucket-top' boots of the period. *Ills. 106 and 107* show the development of the falling collar

Women's clothes, although still elaborate, were more natural, in that the female body was not so much deformed as it had been by tight-lacing and the cumbrous farthingale. Women benefited, too, by the transition from the ruff to the falling collar, and this tendency was even more apparent after the assassination of Henry IV and the accession of Louis XIII.

Ill. 108

Fortunately we have a valuable documentation of the costume of this period in the engravings of Abraham Bosse. Scholars are agreed that they are not fanciful but give a faithful picture of the modes and manners of the time. From these engravings and from the etchings of Jacques Callot we can gain a very clear idea of the costume which in France is associated with *The Three Musketeers* and in England was the dress of the 'Cavaliers'. There was about it an element of martial swagger, with its breeches and doublet, its short cloak hanging from

Ills. 105–7, 109

104

109 *Gallery of the Palais Royal*, full of stalls selling every kind of finery. Engraving by Abraham Bosse, c. 1640

one shoulder, its wide-brimmed hat adorned with a plume and, above all, its boots. These could be of various forms, but the most characteristic style was that of the so-called 'funnel boots', with wide turnovers sometimes trimmed with lace. These were really riding boots, but from about 1610 they were frequently worn in town and indoors.

When shoes were worn, they were decorated with enormous rosettes, made of ribbons, lace and spangles and often extremely costly. Women's shoes were simpler, being almost completely concealed by the long skirt. In wet weather *chopines* were worn. These were wooden clogs covered with leather, worn under the shoes and sometimes with soles thick enough to qualify as stilts. They had been known since the beginning of the century (and in Venice from a much earlier date), as we can gather from Hamlet's remark: 'Your ladyship is nearer heaven than when I saw you last, by the altitude of a chopine.'

110 *Henry Rich, 1st Earl of Holland*, studio of Daniel Mytens, 1640. The new passion for lace, worn at the sitter's throat and, more inventively, in the tops of his boots

111 *Wedding celebration*, by Wolfgang Heimbren, 1637

Women's dress consisted of the bodice, the petticoat and the gown. The bodice was sometimes extravagantly décolleté and laced with a silk ribbon in front. The lacing was often covered with a 'piece' or 'plastron'. The sleeves were large, slashed or paned, and puffed out with stuffing. The character-istic skirt of the period was in fact two skirts, the over-skirt being gathered up to reveal the skirt underneath. The falling collar became ever more elaborate, with a border of costly lace.

Hair was generally worn rather flat on the top of the head, but frizzed out at the sides in thick curls. Women in general did not wear hats, but out of doors they provided themselves with little hoods of black taffeta or else wore a simple lace fichu on their heads.

What we have been describing were in effect French modes. In England they were copied, as we have noted, by the Cavaliers. The Puritans on the other hand, tended to derive their fashions (if such a frivolous word may be allowed in this connection) from Holland.

The system of government of the Protestant Netherlands was different from that obtaining elsewhere in Europe. Holland was ruled by a prosperous *bourgeoisie*, a body of influential and pious merchants and magistrates known as 'regents'. They wore a distinctive costume of conservative cut and black in hue. There is a paradox in this, for the Dutch had fought bitterly to obtain their freedom from Spain, and yet the formality and sobriety of their costume continued to show a Spanish influence. Indeed, it seemed to them suitable raiment for their own austere brand of Protestantism. But the most striking thing

112 Left, *Autumn*, after W. Hollar, *c.* 1650

113 The persistence of the ruff: *Portrait of a middle-aged woman with hands folded*, by Frans Hals, 1633

about Dutch costume in the first half of the seventeenth century is the persistence of the ruff. It not only persisted; it grew larger and larger until it became a literal cartwheel of elaborately *Ill. 113* goffered linen folds, as can be seen in the portraits of Frans Hals. The English Puritans never copied this fashion. Many Dutchmen, however, wore their hair short, and this became the characteristic of the Parliament men in England: hence the nickname 'Roundheads'.

We gain a charming glimpse of English fashions in the middle of the century from the engravings of Wenzel Hollar. Women wore their hair flat on the top of the head, with side curls or ringlets. The bodice was cut low, but with a linen kerchief or collar, which was sometimes transparent. The three-quarter-length sleeves had turn-ups of lace. The bodice came to a deep point and was laced down the front with visible ribbons. The skirt fell in folds to the ground. The general effect *Ill. 112* might be described as a stylish modesty.

But the strange and, according to the moralists, immodest fashion had already arrived of wearing patches on the face. The satirist John Bulwer in his *Artificial Changeling*, published in 1653, ridicules the ladies' 'vain custom of spotting their faces out of an affectation of a mole, to set off their beauty, such as Venus had; and it is well if one patch will serve to make their faces remarkable, for some fill their visages full of them, varied into all manner of shapes'. Such shapes might be stars, crescents or even a coach and horses, cut out of black 'court plaster'. This strange fashion lasted for more than fifty years.

The Restoration of Charles II in 1660 brought with it the triumph of French modes, although significant differences continued to exist between the clothes worn in France and those worn in England. The fashions which Charles brought with him and which were adopted by his Court were among the strangest male garments ever worn. Subsequent historians have regarded them with an unfavourable eye. 'Taste and elegance', says F. W. Fairholt, 'were abandoned for extravagance and folly; and the male costume, which in the time of

Charles I had reached the highest point of picturesque splendour, degenerated and declined from this moment.' *(Costume in England,* 1885.)

Randle Holme, writing in 1684, described men's clothes as consisting of 'short-waisted doublets and petticoat breeches, the lining lower than the breeches, tied above the knee, ribbons up to pocket-holes half the length of the breeches, then ribbons all about the waistband, the shirt hanging out' *(Accidents of Armoury).* The petticoat breeches were a French fashion, or rather had become French, having been introduced by a certain Comte de Salm, known as 'the Rhinegrave'. The breeches were therefore called 'Rhinegraves' and were first worn in England, two years before the Restoration, by William Ravenscroft. They were then regarded as something of a curiosity, but after 1660 they became for a time universal among men with any pretension to fashion. They were so wide that, as Samuel Pepys tells us in an entry in his *Diary* for 1661, it was possible to put both legs into one compartment.

Ill. 114

114 Suit with petticoat breeches, *c.* 1665

116 Sir Thomas Isham's wedding suit, *c.* 1681

The two suits show the transition from doublet with petticoat breeches to the 'vest' 'after the Persian mode', seen for the first time at Court in 1666

115 *Two ladies of the Lake family*, by Peter Lely, c. 1660

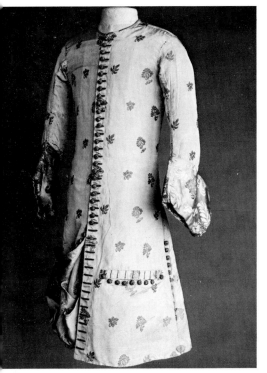

111

The extremely short doublet, so short that it showed a gap of shirt between its lower edge and the top of the breeches, was now buttoned down the front and resembled a sleeved waistcoat. There was a mania for bunches of ribbon, worn not only on the breeches but on the shoulders and elsewhere. We hear of a suit and cloak of satin, trimmed with thirty-six yards of silver ribbon, and no less than 250 yards of ribbon in bunches were used on one pair of petticoat breeches. The general effect of men's clothes at this period was of a fantastic negligence, well suited to the moral climate of the Restoration Court.

Ill. 115 Women's clothes were equally loose and apparently careless, so that most of the Court beauties painted by Lely seem to have been caught, as it were, in *négligé*, although some allowance must no doubt be made for the painter's poetic fancy. The style had its own attractiveness and even the sober Planché is moved to enthusiasm. 'A studied negligence,' he says, 'an elegant déshabille, is the prevailing character of the costume in which they are nearly all represented; their glossy ringlets escaping from a simple bandeau of pearls or adorned by a single rose, fall in graceful profusion upon many necks unveiled by even the transparent lawn of the band or the partlet; and the fair round arm, bare to the elbow, reclines upon the voluptuous satin petticoat while the gown of the same rich material piles up its voluminous train in the background.' (*A Cyclopaedia of Costume*, vol. II 1879, pl. 242.)

There was not much change in female dress during the greater part of Charles II's reign. The long pointed waists continued and gradually became tighter. The tucked-up skirts, known, confusingly, as *manteaux*, grew more formal in appearance, the general outline of the figure stiffer and narrower. The large collars of lace went out of fashion in the early 1670s, although, out of doors, a kerchief called a 'palatine' covered the bare shoulders. But while women's clothes remained comparatively static, those worn by men underwent a real revolution, the ultimate consequences of which can still be seen in modern dress.

112

117 *Charles II on horseback*, by Pieter Stevensz, *c.* 1670. The King is in the new fashion with lace *rabat*, full-bottomed wig and plumed hat anticipating the *tricorne*

It is strange that the name of Charles II, of all people, should *Ill. 117* be associated with a 'reform' of dress. Perhaps he was sobered for a moment by the plague and fire that had just devastated his capital, but, at all events, within little more than a month of the extinguishing of the fire, he took the step which provoked so much comment in contemporary diaries and memoirs. 'In this month', we read in Rugge's *Diurnal* for 11 October 1666, 'his Magestie and whole Court changed the fashion of their clothes, viz., a close coat of cloth pinkt, with a white taffety under the cutts. This in length reached the calf of the leg, and upon that a surcoat cutt at the breast which hung loose and shorter than the vest six inches. The breeches, the Spanish cut, and buskins some of cloth, some of leather, but of the same colour as the vest or garment.'

Pepys, too, describes the new dress and is even more precise in his dates. On 8 October 1666 he notes in his *Diary*: 'The King hath yesterday in Council declared his resolution of setting a fashion of clothes which he will never alter.' On 15 October he comments: 'This day the King begins to put on his vest, and I did see several persons of the House of Lords and Commons too, great courtiers, who are in it; being a long cassocke close to the body, of black cloth, and pinked with white silke under it, and a coat over it, and the legs ruffled with black riband like a pigeon's leg; and, upon the whole, I wish the King may keep it, for it is a very fine and handsome garment.'

Evelyn's *Diary* is equally explicit. Under the date 18 October, he remarks: 'To Court, it being the first time his Majesty put himself solemnly into the Eastern fashion of vest, changing doublet, stiff collar, bands and cloak, into a comely dress after the Persian mode, with girdles or straps, and shoestrings and garters into buckles, of which some were set with precious stones, resolving never to alter it, and to leave the French mode, which had hitherto obtained to our great expense and reproach. Upon which divers courtiers and gentlemen gave his Majesty gold by way of wager that he would not persist in this resolution.'

Charles, however, did persist – but he made certain modifications. Pepys notes (17 October 1666) that 'the Court is full of vests, only my Lord St Albans not pinked but plain black; and they say the King says the pinking upon white makes them look too much like magpies, and therefore hath bespoke one of plain velvet.' Evelyn described the new garment as a 'dress after the Persian mode', and as 'the Eastern fashion of vest'. Other contemporary references call the new fashion 'Turkish'; and one has to admit that it does bear a certain resemblance to the Persian coat except that the latter had long sleeves, whereas the sleeves of Charles's 'vest' were extremely short, the white shirt sleeve ballooning out below it.

Curiously enough the Persian coat was not entirely unknown

at the English Court, Sir Robert Shirley having regularly worn   *Ill. 118*
it as long before as the reign of Charles I. Shirley, who had
travelled much in Persia in the early years of the seventeenth
century, occupied the strange position, for an Englishman, of
Persian Ambassador at the Court of St James's. English relations
with Persia were, indeed, very close throughout the century;
and a new fillip to English interest in the East was given when
Charles II received the island of Bombay as part of the dowry
of Catherine of Braganza.

115

The English King's action was looked upon as a deliberate attempt to break away from French fashions, a step that was hardly likely to please Louis XIV, who was then endeavouring, with considerable success, to make France the arbiter of Europe, not only politically but also in matters of taste. Pepys notes (22 November 1666) that 'the King of France hath, in defiance to the King of England, 'caused all his footmen to be put into vests, and that the noblemen of France will do the like; which, if true, is the greatest indignity ever done by one prince to another'. French scholars, however, have pointed out that a very similar garment was introduced at the French Court as early as 1662. It was at first worn only by a few privileged courtiers, but by 1670 its use had become universal.

How did it come about that this Persian mode became the ancestor of modern costume? Richard Heath notes that 'over the vest a loose overcoat was worn; but, since all reference to it is omitted by Evelyn, and Pepys speaks of seeing the Court full of vests, it was evidently only intended for outdoor wear' ('Studies in English Costume I', *Magazine of Art*, vol. XI, 1887–8). It can be seen, worn as an overcoat, in a contemporary engraving of the funeral of General Monck in 1670. In the end the overcoat became the coat, and the vest became what was later, when it had grown much shorter, to be called the waistcoat. It is interesting to note that London bespoke tailors still refer to a waistcoat as a 'vest'.

Ills. 119, 120   At first it was extremely long, almost as long as the coat, coming nearly to the knees and buttoned all the way down, almost completely concealing the breeches. The coat was rather plain, embroidery being reserved for the inner garment, and the wide falling collar disappeared, since the coat made it inconvenient. Instead a cravat of lace or muslin was worn.

There has been considerable controversy about the origin of this item of apparel. The name seems to imply that it was derived from the neckwear of the Croats in the French service and that it was copied first by the French officers and then by the courtiers of Louis XIV. A fine-lace industry had been

119 *Duke of Burgundy*, by R. Bonnart, *c.* 1695

120 Viol player, by J. D. de Saint-Jean, 1695. The full-bottomed wig is now universal in polite society

established in France by the enlightened minister Colbert, and the King, anxious to encourage it, wore its products himself and decreed that nothing but *point de France* should be worn at Court. The well-known expert on old lace, Mrs Nevill Jackson, writing in *The Connoisseur*, remarks that 'the neckwear of a gentleman of fashion which immediately preceded the cravat was the rabat or falling collar, which in its turn had ousted the ruff, so that we are not surprised to find that the earliest cravats hang like the fronts of a turn-down collar, and are guiltless of bow or knot'.

121 Lady of Quality, by J. D. de Saint-Jean, 1693
122 Lady of Quality, *en déshabille*, by J. D. de Saint-Jean, 1687

Point de France, and the even more elaborate *point de Venise*, was extremely costly. We learn from the Great Wardrobe Accounts that Charles II paid £20. 12s. 0d. for a new cravat, and James II paid £30. 10s. 0d. for one to be worn at his own Coronation. These were very considerable sums in those days.

Towards the end of the seventeenth century the cravat had become narrower and longer. A bow of ribbon was sometimes worn behind it, and the cravat itself (no longer made of lace but of muslin or cambric) was sometimes knotted. At the Battle of Steinkirk in 1692 the French officers, summoned to repel a surprise attack, had no time to arrange their cravats properly. They accordingly twisted them quickly, drawing them through a buttonhole to keep them out of the way.

TOUT CE QUI RELUIT N'EST PAS OR.

Mode dimiter les gens de qualité autant que faire se peut

Mode de trousser juppes et manteau jusqu'aux épaules

Une belle apparence soutient le credit

mode d'être aussi braue que Savoisine

Mode d'aller en pantoufle par la ville

Mode de faire voir le bas de soye Et là jarretiere à frange d'Or

123 *Mode bourgeoise*, by N. Guérard, *c.* 1690. The dress is remarkable for the profusion of lace with which it is trimmed. The high *fontange* is also of lace. The skirt is lifted to display the silk stockings

Ill. 120   This was the origin of the 'steinkirk' which became a prevalent mode for about a dozen years not only in France but all over Europe.

We have noted that the old style of falling collar was inconvenient to wear with the new kind of 'vest'. It therefore shrank to a rabat; but another reason for its diminution in size was that the greater part of a falling collar would have been invisible anyway owing to the custom of wearing a periwig. In the preceding reign the prevailing fashion for long hair no doubt caused many gentlemen to provide themselves with *postiches*, but the effect aimed at was that of natural hair. By 1660, however, the periwig had become frankly artificial and it was adopted with such enthusiasm that no less than two hundred *perruquiers* were employed at the French Court.

The English Court took a little time to catch up, but by November 1663 Pepys was able to note in his *Diary*: 'I heard the Duke [of York] say that he was going to wear a periwig and they say the King also will. I never till this day observed

124, 125 Middle- and working-class costume, by S. le Clerc, end of seventeenth century

that the King is mighty gray.' And in the entry for 15 February 1664 he remarks: 'To White Hall, to the Duke; where he first put on a periwig today: but methought his hair cut short in order thereto did look very pretty of itself, before he put on his periwig.' It was of course necessary to cut the hair close to the scalp, or even to shave it, to make the periwig fit.

In April 1664 he went to Hyde Park and 'saw the King with his periwig'. Pepys had already decided to adopt the new fashion, and one can't help feeling that he was a little disappointed at not making more of a sensation by wearing it when he went to church in it for the first time: 'I found that my coming in a periwig did not prove so strange as I was afraid it would for I thought that all the church would presently have set their eyes upon me.' The invaluable diarist tells us that in 1667 he paid £4. 10s. 0d. for two periwigs, and that a year later he arranged with his barber to keep his periwigs in good order for 20s. per annum. But of course the periwigs worn by the courtiers were much more expensive.

126, 127 Aristocratic costumes, by S. le Clerc, end of seventeenth century

The full-bottomed wig worn by men of fashion was extremely large and heavy, and active persons such as soldiers soon found it an encumbrance. We hear of a 'campaign' wig and a 'travelling' wig. The strange thing is that a wig of some kind was considered absolutely essential and that the fashion should have lasted, for the upper classes of Western Europe, for nearly a century.

Even more curious than the wearing of mountains of artificial hair was the use of powder. This certainly did not originate with Louis XIV, who disapproved of it and only adopted it when it had become a universal fashion at the end of his reign. The periwig of Charles II was black and remained so, and, from their portraits, it seems unlikely that either William III or Queen Anne ever wore powder. Indeed, powder does not come into general use until the 1690s. Pepys, whose *Diary* stops too soon, does not mention it at all. Evelyn, however, speaks of it in his *Mundus Muliebris*, published in 1694, but in this he was, of course, satirizing female fashions. The most definite evidence of the use of hair-powder by Englishmen is to be obtained from the dramatists of the period. Colley Cibber, in his famous comedy *Love's Last Shift* (1695) speaks of 'a cloud of powder beaten out of a beau's periwig'.

Women did not wear the periwig, but they aspired to the same lofty heights in their headdress by the invention of the *fontange*, so characteristic of the 1690s. It was named after one of the favourites of Louis XIV who, the story goes, finding her hair disarranged while hunting, tied it up hastily with one of her garters. The King expressed his admiration, and the mode was launched. Next day all the Court ladies appeared with their hair tied with a ribbon with the bow in front. The fashion quickly crossed the Channel and is one of the earliest examples of a French mode imposing itself on England, universally and almost at once.

Soon a simple bow of ribbon was not enough. Lace was added, and then a cap was added to the lace, with a wire frame to support the ever increasing height of the structure. It was

128 *James Stuart and his sister Louisa Maria Theresa*, by Largillière, 1695

then called, perhaps in irony, a 'commode', and in England was known also as a 'tower'. In the *Ladies Dictionary* of 1694 it is described as 'a frame of wire two or three stories high, fitted to the head, and covered with tiffany or other thin silks being now compleated into the whole headdress'. Moralists, as usual, regarded the new fashion with grave misgiving, as an incitement to pride, and Samuel Wesley the Elder, father of the more famous John Wesley, once preached a sermon against it, from the text: 'Let him that is upon the house-top not come down', drawing particular attention to the words 'Top-knot, come down.'

Various accounts are given of the derivation of the fashion and of the reasons for its disappearance. Louis XIV had grown tired of it by 1699 and expressed his disapproval, but it was the appearance at Court of an Englishwoman, Lady Sandwich, 'avec une petite coiffure basse', which really changed the mode. This must have been a personal eccentricity on the part of Lady Sandwich, for in general French fashions were dropped in England some time after they had been abandoned in France. We find the *Mercure Galant* for November 1699 remarking that the old style of high coiffure was beginning to appear ridiculous. Some ten years later Addison was commenting upon its final disappearance in England.

The male hat assumed, in the closing years of the seventeenth century, the shape it was to keep throughout the eighteenth. The hat of the Commonwealth, whether worn by Roundhead or by Cavalier (the latter wore it with a feather), was distinguished by its high crown and wide brim. Charles II brought in the so-called 'French hat', with wide brim and shallower crown, adorned with even more feathers than before. At the funeral of General Monck in 1670, already referred to, the hats are very small in brim also. Finally the crown settled down to a moderate height, and the brim, which had become wide again, underwent the process known as 'cocking' – that is to say, one portion of it was turned up either at the front, at the back or on one side of the head.

At first this seems to have been a matter of individual fancy: we hear, for instance, of the 'Monmouth cock'. In the reign of William and Mary the hat began to be turned up in three places, thus forming the 'three-cornered hat' which lasted for a century and was accepted as the only possible headgear for gentlemen throughout the civilized world. 'The cocked hat,' says Planché (*Cyclopaedia*, vol. I, 1876, p. 260), 'was considered as a mark of gentility, professional rank, and distinction from the lower orders who wore them uncocked.' Such differences as there were depended upon the width of the brim, the largest being known as the 'Kevenhuller'.

Hats, strangely enough, were worn indoors and even at dinner; it was only in the presence of Royalty that gentlemen went bare-headed. The hat and the periwig were symbolic of the extreme formality of manners that marked the closing years of the seventeenth century.

129 Wedding procession, from *Relazione del regno di Svezia* by Lorenzo Magalotti, 1674. The hat has begun to be cocked, but has not yet become the *tricorne*

130 *Madame de Pompadour*, by François Boucher, 1759

The eighteenth century

THE ESSENTIAL lines of eighteenth-century costume were, as we have noted in the previous chapter, already laid down in the last twenty years of the seventeenth. The enormous prestige of the Court of Versailles had already resulted, all over Europe, in a willingness to accept, in matters of fashion as in much else, the dominance of France. Henceforward fashionable clothes meant, for the upper classes at least, French clothes.

Versailles, however, was no longer the Court of a young King, avid for pleasure, but of an ageing monarch whose thoughts were turning to piety. Madame de la Vallière and Madame de Montespan had been replaced by the *dévote* Madame de Maintenon, and this change was reflected even in the courtiers' clothes. So far as materials were concerned, they were rich and splendid enough, but the easy, flowing lines of the earlier modes had given place to a new ideal of propriety and *tenue*. The general effect was of rigidity, dignity and serious-ness. The new headdress for women – the *fontange*, which built up the hair into a peak crowned by a high cap – increased the apparent height and added to the vertical effect.

The same appearance of dignity was obtained by men, from 1680 onwards, by the *perruque à crinière* or full-bottomed wig. We have already dealt with the first appearance, at the Court of Louis XIV and the Court of Charles II, of the wig worn, not to conceal the lack of natural hair, but as an essential item in the dress of every upper-class man. It began to be powdered in the early years of the eighteenth century, and this strange custom persisted until the French Revolution.

The full-bottomed wig was an extremely cumbrous affair, and very expensive. It formed a mass of curls framing the face

131, 132 The full-bottomed wig of Lord Mohun, *c.* 1710 (right), has become in a generation the formalized wig of Martin Folkes, *c.* 1740 (left)

and falling below the shoulders. Fops wore it even longer. Until about 1710 it was also very high above the forehead. At home it was often replaced by an embroidered cap, and literary men and philosophers are sometimes shown in contemporary portraits as bare-headed but with their hair cropped close.

It was quite impracticable for any active pursuit, and soldiers soon evolved what was known as the 'campaign' wig. This continued to have a mass of curls but arranged in three locks of hair, one at the back and one at each side of the face, the ends being turned up and tied in a knot. The 'Ramillies wig' (called after Marlborough's victory over the French in 1706) was a further simplification. The hair was drawn back and tied in a long pigtail, generally with two bows of black ribbon, one at the top of the pigtail and a smaller one at the bottom.

128

133 *The five orders of periwigs*, by William Hogarth, 1761

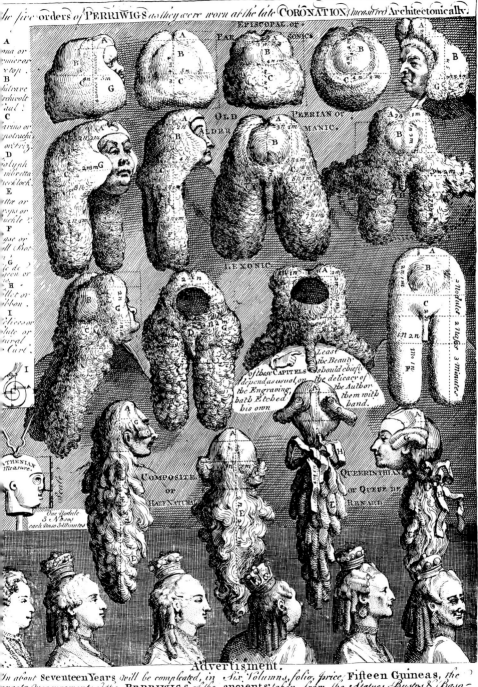

On informal occasions men wore the bob wig, with the hair ending in a roll round the back of the neck. Clergymen and scholars affected a bob wig which was frizzed rather than curled. They also wore the 'tye' wig, with the hair drawn back into a queue tied with black ribbon. In the 'bag' wig this queue was enclosed in a square black bag or pouch, made of silk. The wig itself was sometimes black, but in general it was covered with white or grey powder. It could be made of human hair (this, naturally, being the most expensive) or of goat's hair, horsehair or vegetable fibres. Women, in general, did not wear wigs but powdered their own hair, sometimes added to by means of false curls worn at the back of the head.

The closing years of the reign of Louis XIV were marked by an increase, if that were possible, in stiffness and formality, but his death in 1715 opened a new era. As if in reaction against all that the Roi Soleil had stood for, women's clothes became looser and with more flowing lines. A contemporary notes in the magazine *La Bagatelle*, 1718, that 'at present comfort seems the only thing that the ladies of Paris care about when dressing'.

Ills. 134–6 The new form of dress was called a 'sack' or 'sacque', a comfortable, rather shapeless garment, with small box pleats behind. When these were double or treble and descended from the neck, merging below the shoulders into the folds of the gown, they were known as the 'sackback'. A more usual name is the 'Watteau pleat'. Scholars have attacked the term as erroneous, but it is certainly true that nearly all the ladies in Watteau's pictures are wearing it.

A curious feature of the clothes of this period was the return of hoops. Instead of height women now seemed to aim at width, and the skirt was distended sideways, sometimes to as much as fifteen feet, by means of whalebone or rods of osier. Hence the word *panier*, the French for 'basket', which the underlying structure of the skirt somewhat resembled. The extreme width of women's dresses at this period was the cause of some

Ill. 140 inconvenience, since it was impossible for two ladies to pass through a door side by side or even sit on the same couch. The

134, 135 The 'sack'. Left, *Lady Howard*, after Godfrey Kneller, *c.* 1710; right, *Mrs Anastasia Robinson*, after Vanderbank, *c.* 1723

fashion even had an effect on architecture, for example in the curved balusters of eighteenth-century staircases.

The classification of women's dresses at this period is a matter of some difficulty. Modern scholars have suggested a general division into 'open' robes and 'closed' robes, while acknowledging that such terms were never used at the time. The closed robe was a dress consisting of a bodice and petticoat (sometimes forming one garment) with no opening in the front of the skirt. The more characteristic open robe had a gap in the front of the skirt, in the shape of an inverted V, which allowed the petticoat to be seen beneath. This petticoat was sometimes quilted and sometimes embroidered even more lavishly than the skirt itself.

There was a similar arrangement of the bodice, which had a gap in front filled in by means of a stomacher shaped like a

131

shield and stiffened with pasteboard or busks. It was often
heavily embroidered or decorated with a series of bows decreasing in size from top to bottom. The bodice was usually
laced behind, and stiffened with whalebone.

The characteristic eighteenth-century sleeve ended just
above or just below the elbow and was wide enough for the
chemise-sleeve to emerge from it, with its ruffle of lace. Sometimes the ruffles were double or treble, the upper ones being
slightly shorter so as to display the lace to better advantage. It
was fashionable to match the lace on the ruffle with that on the
cap and tucker. The latter was the white, frilled edging to the
bodice, originally part of the shift but often sewn on separately.
The 'modesty piece' had a similar function, that of concealing
the lower part of the décolletage. The handkerchief, sometimes
called a 'neckerchief', was a large square of linen, muslin or
silk, folded and draped round the neck. (In fact, both terms are
etymologically absurd, since the word 'kerchief', *couvre-chef*,
originally meant a covering for the head.) There was also a

136 Sketches by Antoine Watteau

137 Costumes for a lady and her maid, from *La Couturière*, mid eighteenth century

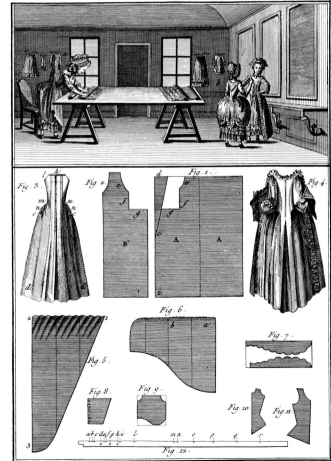

138 Workroom of a dressmaker and diagrams to show the method of cutting, from the *Encyclopédie Méthodique*, 1748

version known as the 'half handkerchief', for informal occasions.

For three-quarters of the eighteenth century there was no essential change in the male mode established in the middle years of the reign of Louis XIV. Male dress consisted of coat, waistcoat and breeches. The coat was close-fitting to the waist and then flared out in skirts of varying length. It had three vents, one at the back and one at each side, the last two being pleated. The coat was either collarless or was provided with a narrow, upright band. There was a row of buttons down the front of the coat, but most of these were left unfastened. The

139 *The Graham children*, by William Hogarth, 1742. There is hardly any distinction between children's clothes and adult attire

140 *Mr and Mrs Andrews*, by Thomas Gainsborough, *c.* 1748. The gentleman is in informal country attire but the lady is wearing the extremely
wide paniers of the current mode

sleeves were of great importance, and it is often possible to
date clothes by the gradual diminution in the size of the cuffs
as the century progressed. At first they were extremely large,
being turned back and buttoned either just below or just above
the elbow. Beneath the cuff showed the ruffle of the shirt, the
lace used matching the lace of the shirt front.

Beneath the coat was the waistcoat, of different material and
sometimes heavily embroidered. After the middle of the century the embroidery spread to the coat itself. In the early
years of the century the waistcoat was almost as long as the
coat and, like it, was furnished with buttons all the way down.
The lower buttons were never fastened. It was close-fitting to
the waist and then flared out in skirts with unpleated vents,
often stiffened with buckram. The back of the waistcoat was
made of less expensive material.

135

Knee-breeches were universally worn throughout the century. They were fairly loose and fitted over the hips without the need of either belt or braces. They were closed below the knee with three or four buttons, and at first the stockings were drawn over them. From about 1735, however, the breeches, closed with an ornamental buckle, were worn over the stockings.

Neckwear continued, without much variation, the tradition of the late seventeenth century, that is the cravat or the steinkirk described in the previous chapter; but from about 1740 younger men began to wear a stock, consisting of a piece of linen or cambric sometimes stiffened with pasteboard and buckled behind. Sometimes there was worn with it a black tie known as a 'solitaire'. This was usually worn with the bag wig.

141 *Two ladies sewing, c.* 1750

142 *Joseph Suss,* 1738

143 *Lady with straw hat,* by C. W. E. Dietrich, *c.* 1750

The three-cornered hat was almost universal throughout the
century, although country people and scholars sometimes wore
their hats uncocked. The usual practice was to turn up the brim
and attach it to the low crown in such a way as to form a triangle.
The brim was usually edged with braid, and a button or a jewel
was sometimes fixed to the left cock. The appearance of the
hat was naturally conditioned by the width of the brim. The
so-called 'Kevenhuller hat' had a wide brim, and was fashionable in the 1740s. The same is true of the Dettingen hat (called
after the Battle of Dettingen in 1743). It aimed at an effect of
military swagger. The usual colour of hats was black, although
Beau Nash, 'King of Bath', made himself deliberately conspicuous by wearing a white hat. The material was beaver, a
cheaper variety being made of rabbit fur.

137

144 *Thé à l'Anglaise chez la Princesse de Conti*, by Michel-Barthélemy Ollivier, 1766

145 *Girl with chocolate*, by Jean Etienne Liotard, mid eighteenth century. The girl's costume shows the characteristic time-lag at this period between servants' costume and that of their masters

By the 1760s we can begin to discern the tentative beginnings of a new style. In essence the change consisted of a decreasing emphasis on the French 'Court' style and an increasing adoption of English 'country' clothes. There was, in short, a trend towards practicality and simplicity. Coats were plain, had narrower cuffs and the skirts were sometimes cut away in front for ease on horseback. Even the universal three-cornered hat began to be replaced, at least for such pursuits as hunting, by a narrow-brimmed, high-crowned hat which served as a kind of primitive crash-helmet, and in which we can already see the outline of the top hat of the nineteenth century.

However, the 'macaronis' of the 1770s were a reaction against these developments. They wore very thin shoes with enormous buckles made of gold, silver, pinchbeck or steel and set with real or imitation stones. They affected very large buttons on their coats. Their hats were extremely small, but their wigs were dressed high on the head, prodigiously curled.

*Ills. 148–
51* This was in line with the development of women's hair-dressing at this period. The hair, having been dressed close to the head since the age of the *fontange*, began to rise in the 1760s, and we hear that 'Lady Strathmore's dress is the wonder of the town, her head a yard high and filled, or rather covered with feathers to an enormous size' (Letters of the Hon. Mrs Osborn, 1767). This was probably an exaggeration in the 1760s, but became true in the 1770s. George Colman the Younger describes a contemporary headdress: 'A towering toupee pulled up all but by the roots and strained over a cushion on the top of her head, formed the centre of the building; tiers of curls served for the wings; a hanging chignon behind defended her occiput like a buttress; and the whole fabric was kept tight and water proof by a quantity of long single and double black pins' (*Random Records*, 1770).

140

146 Far left, mob cap, 1780

147, 148 Male and female coiffures, c. 1778

149–152 Three female headdresses and man in a soft hat, c. 1778.

It was at this period that the headdresses of women reached their most exaggerated height. Men, on the other hand, were adopting a more simple style, even discarding the *tricorne*

The 'double pins' mentioned were what we would call hairpins, which came into use just about this time. The 'cushion' was a pad stuffed with tow, wool or horsehair, and because it induced headaches, it was later replaced by a wire frame over which the natural hair was draped, with false hair added. The whole was plastered with pomatum and covered with white powder. Such a structure, which sometimes remained untouched for months, soon became the resort of vermin, and the little ivory claws on the end of a long stick which antique dealers still refer to as 'back scratchers' were really made to insert into the headdress in an endeavour to relieve the intolerable itching.

The headdress was sometimes crowned with the most fantastic objects: a ship in full sail, a windmill with farm animals grouped about it, a garden with real or artificial flowers. Or

153 *The Morning Walk*, by Thomas Gainsborough, 178)

154 *Joseph II meets Catherine the Great*, by J. H. Löschenkohl, 1787

else a hat could be worn. Such hats were rather small in the
early 1770s, but gradually grew larger. Some were of soft
material, some with stiff crowns and wide brims adorned with
feathers, as can be seen in Gainsborough's famous picture, *The
Morning Walk*. This was painted in 1785, by which time the   *Ill. 153*
hair was being dressed broad instead of high, was frizzed
instead of curled and was sometimes enclosed in an enormous
mob cap instead of a hat.

Beginning in the 1770s, there was a marked change in the
general outline of women's dress, which can be summed up as
a transition from hoops to a kind of bustle. The bodice also
began to be puffed out, giving a pouter-pigeon effect. Bodices
were in general deeply décolleté, the gap being filled in with
a neckerchief. Many women adopted a masculine style of

143

155 *N'ayez pas peur, ma bonne amie*, after Moreau le Jeune, *c.* 1776. A visit to the mother-to-be. The gentleman is an abbé. The visiting ladies are wearing the elaborate day clothes and the high headdresses of the period

156 *Les Adieux*, after Moreau le Jeune, *c.* 1777. The lady is entering a box at the Opera in full evening dress with enormous paniers and deep square décolletage

waistcoat, and even a 'great-coat' dress or 'riding-coat' dress with revers and a triple falling collar. Considerable variation in female attire was now possible, as we can see from *La Galerie des Modes*, a pioneer in the field of the fashion plate, published in parts at irregular intervals between 1778 and 1787.

The fashion plate, indeed, sprang into existence at this period, with immense consequences in the dissemination of fashion. As Vyvyan Holland has pointed out in *Hand-coloured Fashion Plates, 1770–1899*, it is important to distinguish the fashion plate from the 'costume plate'. The latter attempts to show clothes 'after the event', as it were, as Wenceslas Hollar did,

157 *Le Rendez-vous pour Marly*, after Moreau le Jeune, *c.* 1776.
Walking dress of considerable elaboration

for example, in his *Ornatus Muliebris Anglicanus*, published in 1640, or as Jean Dieu de Saint-Jean did in France in his admirable engravings of male and female costume at the Court of Louis XIV. Even *Le Monument du Costume* of Freudenberg and Moreau le Jeune, published in Paris between 1775 and 1783, consisted of 'costume plates'.

Curiously enough the first true fashion plates were not French but English. *The Lady's Magazine* was publishing them

146

158 *The Promenade at Carlisle House*, by J. R. Smith, 1781. At this house of assignation the gentlemen wear their hats, the one on the left having abandoned the *tricorne* and adopted 'country' clothes

159 *Coiffure sans redoute, c.* 1785. The headdress, wide instead of high, is very typical of the 1780s. On top is perched the early form of the top hat. It is a sign of female emancipation when women start wearing hats

from 1770 onwards. And suddenly similar plates were being published all over Europe. Accustomed as we are today to fashion illustrations, it is hard for us to realize that, before the invention of the fashion plate, information concerning the latest fashion was so hard to come by that Marie-Antoinette's dressmaker found it worth while to travel the Continent every year in a huge *berline* containing dolls dressed in the latest *modes de Paris*.

It would be very instructive for the student of costume to compare two sets of fashion plates, such as those in *La Galerie des Modes* and those of Heideloff's *Gallery of Fashion* (he would have to do so in some great public library such as that of the Victoria and Albert Museum). Although a gap of a mere ten years separates these two publications, the clothes depicted in them are entirely different. What had happened in the meantime, of course, was the French Revolution.

Like all great social upheavals, this had a profound effect on the clothes of both men and women. The dress of the Ancien Régime was swept away. Suddenly there were no more embroidered coats or brocaded gowns, no more wigs or powdered hair, no more elaborate headdresses, no more *talons rouges*. 'Return to Nature' was the cry, but in the matter of costume this is never quite possible, unless people are willing to adopt the nudity of the savage. What, then, actually happened?

Ills. 160–63

160, 161 The newly invented fashion plate: *Galerie des Modes, c.* 1778. Left, *Robe à la Polonaise*; right, dressmaker setting out to visit a client and carrying a pair of paniers

In male dress the quest for simplicity meant the abandonment of French 'Court' clothes and the acceptance of English country clothes. For a variety of historical reasons the English upper classes had never been content to flutter round a Court, like their French counterparts. They preferred to spend their time on their country estates. And for active pursuits such as fox-hunting they soon found that they were compelled to adopt a simpler form of dress from that considered fashionable in the capitals of Europe. They took all the embroidery off their coats and had them made of plain cloth. They abolished the lace ruffles at wrist and throat, put aside the white silk stockings and fitted their legs into stout boots. And, as we have already noted, for the universal three-cornered hat they substituted a primitive form of 'topper'.

Now, even before the French Revolution, there was much enthusiasm, even in France, for all things English. England was looked upon as a land of liberty (which indeed, by comparison,

162, 163 Walking and summer dresses, from Heideloff's *Gallery of Fashion*, 1795. Heideloff, a Swiss, was driven out of France by the Revolution and published his great work in England

Fig. 99. Fig. 100.

164 Day dresses, 1796. Fashion plate from Heideloff's *Gallery of Fashion*.
Plumes were worn in the hair even when walking in the country

165 *Point de Convention*, by Louis-Léopold Boilly, *c.* 1801. Even Frenchmen
have now adopted English 'country' clothes

it was), and the result was a wave of anglomania which found
its full expression when the privileges of the French nobility
had been swept away. During the Terror, of course, it was
dangerous to wear fashionable clothes of any kind, but after
the execution of Robespierre, those who had survived the
guillotine began once more to dress as they pleased. And what
they were pleased to wear was a fantasticated version of English
country clothes. The Englishman's hunting coat was given *Ill. 165*
tails of extravagant length, boots of extraordinary shapes
replaced shoes, waistcoats became extremely short, collars rose
to a great height behind the head, and neckcloths became so
voluminous that they sometimes rose over the chin and even

166, 167 Morning dress of 1799 and ball dress of 1800

concealed the mouth. Wigs were abandoned, and the un-
powdered hair was worn in a wild mop sometimes brushed
forward over the forehead. Few more bizarre silhouettes have
ever been seen than those of the French *Incroyables* of the 1790s.

Women's dress at this period was less extravagant, but
showed an even more drastic break with the past. Paniers,
bustles and corsets were all abandoned, as were also the rich
materials of which dresses had formerly been made. Instead
women wore a *robe en chemise*, which did indeed look like an
undergarment, for it consisted of a white, high-waisted muslin
cambric or calico garment falling to the feet and sometimes so
transparent that it was necessary to wear white, or pink, tights
underneath. Sometimes the material was dampened so that it
clung to the body in imitation of the folds of the Greek dresses
represented in antique statues. Heelless slippers contributed to
this effect. Hairdressing was simplified with a similar intention,

but the effect was somewhat spoilt by the plumes of ostrich feathers which it was fashionable to stick in the hair. These were worn even in the daytime, but it should be emphasized that there was at this period very little difference between 'full dress' and 'morning dress' except in the quality of the materials. One curious result of the extreme flimsiness of women's clothes at this time was that pockets in the garments themselves became impracticable. Hence the appearance of a little handbag known as the 'reticule', or 'ridicule', which women began to carry about with them everywhere they went.

In France the accession of Napoleon to power put an end to the extravagance of male fashion under the Directoire. Englishmen had never adopted these strange modes, and by 1800 had settled down to a tightened and smartened version of country clothes: a top hat, a not too exaggerated neckcloth, a coat with revers and a collar of medium height, made of plain cloth and cut away in the front, a waistcoat, not as short as it had been in the 1790s, breeches with a square flap and diagonal side-pockets, and breeches fitting into riding boots. In the evening, pumps, knee-breeches and silk stockings were worn, and a *bicorne* was carried under the arm. The English had been slower than the French to abandon hair-powder, but when the Government imposed a tax on it in 1795, it ceased to be worn except by some of the older men. The pig-tail was given up except by the military, who kept it for another ten years.

In fact, by the end of the eighteenth century the general lines of costume were already laid down: for women a version of what came to be known as the 'Empire' gown; for men a costume which we can already recognize as that of 'John Bull'. These two modes, male and female, showed very little variation all over Europe. One is struck again by the fact that, since the seventeenth century, West European culture has been basically one, and that therefore there is little differentiation in the costume of the various nations, so far, at least, as the upper classes are concerned.

153

CHAPTER SEVEN

From 1800 to 1850

PERHAPS at no period between primitive times and the 1920s had women worn so little as they wore in the early years of the nineteenth century. All female attire seemed to have been designed for tropical climates, and yet the climate of Europe can have been no different in 1800 from what it was in 1850, when women wore ten times as many clothes. In France and England, the leaders in fashion, the accepted garb was a kind of light nightdress reaching, it is true, to the ankles but extremely décolleté even in the daytime. Ruffs came into the mode again, and there was a passion for shawls. Such shawls came *Ill. 172* originally from Cashmere, but the war with England made it difficult for the French to import them, and they therefore began to manufacture similar shawls of their own. Great Britain, too, began to produce imitation Cashmere shawls at Paisley. It was considered the mark of the fashionable lady to be able to wear a shawl with grace, and it formed an essential part of every woman's wardrobe.

168 Left, *Madame Récamier*, by François Gérard, 1802

169 *I have not learned my book, Mamma*, by Adam Buck, *c.* 1800

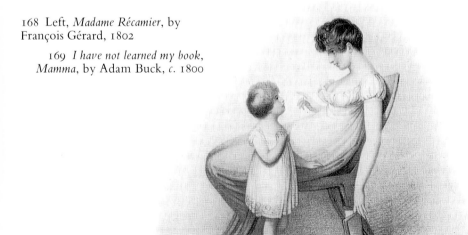

Napoleon's expedition to Egypt had induced in his compatriots a new wave of Orientalism which made turbans fashionable, and these were worn in England as well. Otherwise the outline aimed at a 'classical' effect, with the emphasis on vertical line; but the Oriental influences contributed to modify this ideal, and the classical style only lasted from about 1800 to 1803. An Egyptian influence could be noted for the next three years, and then, owing to the Peninsular War and interest in all things Spanish, gave way to Spanish styles, Spanish ornamentation being superimposed on what was still thought of as a classical garment.

In 1802 there was a cessation of hostilities between England and France, but the Peace of Amiens was short-lived, and for the next twelve years England and France were cut off from one another. When the English ladies flocked over to Paris in 1814 after Napoleon's first abdication, they found to their astonishment that English and French fashions had notably diverged. The French ladies were still wearing white, but the

171 English outdoor dress, c. 1807–10

170 La belle Zélie, by J.-A.-D. Ingres, 1806

172 Male and female walking dress, 1810

173 Summer walking dresses, 1817

Soon after Waterloo, French dresses ceased to be severely 'classical' and, with their heavy flouncing, foreshadowed the style to come

skirt, instead of falling straight to the ankles, now flared out slightly at the hem. English costume, on the other hand, was beginning to look 'romantic', with echoes of such Elizabethan elements as puffed and slashed sleeves. The result of this confrontation was that the English ladies immediately abandoned their insular fashions and adopted French modes.

The exact opposite happened in the case of men's dress. As we have seen, the English influence on male costume was already marked at the end of the eighteenth century, but now

157

174 *Thomas Bewick*, after James Ramsay, *c*. 1810. He wears the cutaway coat and top hat of English country costume, but still has knee-breeches

175 *Captain Barclay*, '*the celebrated pedestrian*', *c*. 1820. Trousers have replaced knee-breeches

176 Male and female walking dress. Fashion plate, 1818

Frenchmen plainly accepted English dress as the law. This was due in no small degree to the superior skill of London tailors, trained to work in wool broadcloth. Such cloth, unlike light silk and other flimsy materials, can be stretched and moulded to the body. The clothes of the eighteenth-century aristocrat were in general very badly made and did not fit at all snugly to the body. Such snug fitting was the very essence of dandyism, and George Brummell prided himself on the fact that his clothes did not show a single wrinkle and that his breeches fitted his legs like a natural skin. Dandyism does not imply gorgeousness in male attire; the exact opposite is the case. There was no embroidery on the dandy's coat; it was made of plain cloth, with the cut-away originally derived from the

158

177 Kensington Garden dresses for June, from *Le Beau Monde*, 1808. An
early example of trousers

KENSINGTON GARDEN DRESSES for June

Engraved exclusively for Le Beau Monde or Library & Fashionable Magazine

hunting coat, and with a preference for the primary colours. Brummell's coat was invariably dark blue, but it was usual to wear waistcoat and breeches of a different colour; for example, a crimson waistcoat and yellow breeches could be worn with a blue coat, or a white waistcoat and sage-green breeches with a black coat. The collar, which stood rather high at the back of the neck, was sometimes of velvet. Waistcoats were in general short and square-cut, with perhaps a couple of inches showing below the front parts of the coat. The upper buttons were left undone to display the frill of the shirt. In Court dress the waistcoat was of white satin embroidered with gold thread.

In the daytime it was usual to wear tight-fitting breeches fitted into riding boots, but in the evening silk stockings were worn with pumps. Some men wore pantaloons or tights with tasselled hessians. Trousers were also worn, but, although close-fitting, did not show the shape of the leg and ended above the ankles. Very wide trousers *à la Turque* were also worn, with an anticipation of the wide trousers which were later to be called 'Cossacks'.

The dandy was shown not only by the cut of his clothes and the snugness of his breeches but by the elaboration of his neckwear. The collar of the shirt was worn upright; the two points projected on to the cheeks and were kept in place by a neckcloth, either in the form of a cravat or a stock. Some dandies were alleged to spend a whole morning in the arrangement of their cravats. Large squares of lawn, muslin or silk, folded cornerwise into a band, were wrapped round the neck and tied in a knot or bow in front. There is the well-known story of a caller visiting Brummell in the middle of the morning and finding his valet arranging his cravat. On the floor was a large heap of discarded cravats, and when the visitor inquired what they were, the valet replied, 'Sir, those are our failures.' The stock was a made-up, stiffened neckband, buckled behind. Since the wearing of either a cravat or a stock made it difficult, if not impossible, to turn or lower the head, it contributed in no small degree to the dandy's imperturbability and hauteur.

178 *Monstrosities of 1822*, by George Cruikshank. Example of exaggerated 'dandy' modes seen in Hyde Park near the statue of Achilles

Top hats of some form were worn at all times of day, but the correct hat for evening was the *bicorne*, in the shape of a crescent, the two brims being pressed against one another, which enabled the hat to be carried under the arm. Hair was short, and it was the fashion to wear it somewhat dishevelled *à la Titus*. Most civilians were clean-shaven, but side-whiskers and occasionally moustaches were worn by military men. The wearing of swords had been entirely abandoned, but it was fashionable to carry a cane; indeed, no well-dressed man was ever seen in the street without one.

Brummell's dress had always been of stolid sobriety, but after his departure in 1819 (he fled to the Continent to escape his creditors) the clothes of the dandies, or those who thought themselves such, began to develop all kinds of extravagances.

179 Walking dress, 1819   180 Carriage dress, 1824

The top hat swelled out at the top until its crown was wider than the brim, the visible ends of the shirt collar came up almost to the eyes, the stock or cravat grew tighter and higher, the shoulders of the coat were padded and the waist nipped in with the aid of a corset. Trousers had now become almost universal, either ending just above the half-boots or strapped under the instep. The caricaturists made merry with this new *Ill. 178* mode, for example in Cruikshank's *Monstrosities of 1822*.

The same year was a turning-point in female dress. The waist, which had been high for a quarter of a century, now resumed its normal position, and when this happens it inevitably becomes tighter and tighter. As a result, the corset once more became an essential element of female dress, even for small girls. A contemporary advertisement advises a mother to make her daughter lie face down on the floor in order that she might

181 French and German costumes, 1826   182 Morning and evening dress, 1831

then place a foot in the small of the back to obtain the necessary purchase on the laces.

The effect of tight-lacing can be increased by widening the skirt and puffing out the sleeves. Both of these were done in the 1820s. Early in the decade the skirts were still fairly narrow, but they were weighted at the bottom by a flounce, frills and other decorations, sometimes even by a band of fur. The sleeves were also modified, first by a little puff at the shoulders, which *Ill. 181* was imagined to be a harking back to the dresses of the Renaissance. The Romantic movement was by now in full swing, the novels of Walter Scott found innumerable readers and every young woman seems to have wanted to look like Amy Robsart or another of his heroines. There was even a vogue for dresses made of Scotch plaid. About 1825 the little puffed sleeve was provided with another sleeve over it, usually

163

183 Male and female riding costume, 1831. The *equestrienne* has masculin-
ized the *upper* half of her costume, but wears a long, trailing skirt

184 Dresses. Fashion plate, 1829

of transparent gauze. When this was made opaque, the sleeve
assumed the curious leg-of-mutton shape so characteristic of
the period. After 1830 the skirt was shorter, but even wider
than before, and the sleeves became enormous.

So did hats. The day cap worn in the home was much
expanded and no longer tied under the chin. Turbans became
extremely wide, so that they no longer looked like turbans but
became veritable hats. The hats themselves were extremely
wide in the brim. Though usually made of straw, they were also
of silk and satin and were trimmed with a mass of flowers,
ribbons and feathers in striking colours. From 1827 onwards
such hats were worn even in the evening at the theatre, making
it almost impossible for anyone sitting behind them to see the
stage. The diarist Croker complains that even at the dinner

185 Pelisse robe, silk brocade, 1831–3. The little puffed sleeve of the late 1820s has become the 'leg of mutton' sleeve of the early 1830s

186 Gentlemen's morning dress, 1834

table the size of the hats of his two companions prevented him from seeing his own plate. Caricaturists of the period delighted to show hats so huge that they served as umbrellas, not only for the wearer but for two companions walking by her side.

Hair was most elaborately arranged, with curls over the forehead and a chignon at the back of the head. Artificial hair was sometimes added in the evening in the form of what was known as the 'Apollo knot', fixed on the top of the head and decorated with flowers, feathers or combs. Some of these were of tortoiseshell set with jewels. Another possible addition was the 'Swiss bodkin', a long hat-pin with a detachable metallic head, derived, it would seem, from the peasant costumes of Switzerland.

After about 1828 skirts became slightly shorter, but sleeves continued to expand. The bodice gave an impression of width.

187 *In the garden*. Fashion plate, 1840. The modest little poke bonnet has replaced the elaborate hats of the previous decade

In the evening it was décolleté, sometimes extremely so, with a straight-across top edge to the corsage. In the daytime it was fashionable to wear a ruff, once more an imitation of what was imagined to have been the Elizabethan mode. A wide, flat collar called a 'pelerine' covered the shoulders. This was some-times provided with hanging ends and was then known as a 'fichu-pelerine'. Out of doors in the daytime women wore a pelisse with enormous sleeves and many capes. With evening dress went various kinds of mantle. Shawls were still worn, but were less fashionable than they had been in the previous decade. In spite of the increased fullness of the skirt, reticules were still carried; muffs were fashionable throughout the decade, although they became somewhat smaller towards its close. A fan was an essential part of the evening toilette, and a

188 *Florence Nightingale and her sister Parthenope*, by W. White, *c.* 1836.
The balloon sleeves, which have now slipped off the shoulder, are about
to vanish altogether

large bouquet was often carried as well. The parasol was another essential part of the fashionable lady's equipment, but it was rarely put up because it would have had to be of enormous size to protect the hat. Instead it was carried in the hand. A great deal of jewellery was worn in the form of lockets, crosses, gold bracelets, mosaic and cameo brooches and gold chains supporting little bottles of perfume.

In 1837 the romantic, flamboyant modes of the first part of the decade began to be modified. Sleeves were no longer so wide, and the bulge had begun to slip down the arm. Skirts were longer again and did not show a woman's ankles when she walked. The boned corsage fitted closely to the body and was adorned in the front with a fan-shaped piece of material. The most striking change was in headgear: tied firmly under the chin, it was no longer a hat but a bonnet. It was worn close to the head in the form of a coal-scuttle and gave an impression of extreme modesty. By comparison with the fashions of the 1830s, indeed, the fashions of the 1840s became positively mouselike. Bright colours gave way to dark greens and browns. Shawls returned to favour. Elaborate hairdressing was abandoned except for the ringlets which framed the face.

Men's clothes, too, became more sombre at this period. Pinched-in waists and padded shoulders were abandoned as well as the flamboyant waistcoats and the dangling seals. The cut-away coat was still worn both in the evening and in the daytime, but in the evening it was now usually black. Many younger men began to prefer the frock coat in the daytime, and in summer the jacket, which had shorter skirts. Frilled shirts vanished from day wear, although they were for a time still fashionable in the evening. The cravat was smaller, although it still kept the shirt collar against the cheek. Sometimes the collar was almost entirely concealed by it. Sportsmen affected spotted neckcloths, kept in place with a pin. The top hat was universally worn by all ranks of society. Its crown was very high at the beginning of the decade, but grew smaller towards its close. In the country a low-crowned informal hat called a

168

'wide-awake' was sometimes worn. Nether garments consisted of trousers, rather tight and strapped under the instep. An alternative was pantaloons, which were tighter still and also strapped under the foot. Breeches were worn in the country, in which case they were made of leather or cord, and also at Court, where they were made of white cassinère. It was unusual for trousers to be made of the same material as coats. Scotch plaids were popular in winter, white drill trousers in summer.

Overcoats of the period show a surprising number of varieties: the top coat, the chesterfield, which was slightly waisted, and the paletot, which was a short coat and could take the place of the overcoat on occasion. The curricle, which was used for driving, had one or several pleats over the shoulders. Cloaks were worn over evening dress. The overcoats worn in France and Germany were essentially English in origin.

The anonymous author of a book on etiquette entitled *The Habits of Good Society*, published in the 1840s, tells us that the well-dressed man needed four kinds of coat: a morning coat, a frock coat, a dress coat and an overcoat. He needed four of the first and one each of the others, the cost of the seven coats being £18 (i.e. little more than £2 each). In addition he needed six pairs of morning and one of evening trousers, at a total cost of £9; and four morning waistcoats and one evening waistcoat, costing £4 in all. Another £10 was to be allowed for gloves, linen, hats, scarves and neckties, and £5 for boots. The well-dressed man of moderate means could therefore fit himself out for under £50 a year, which by modern standards seems extremely little. Of course the dandies, who still persisted into the 1840s, spent very much more than this. They were regarded as relics of a former, dissipated age. The dominant figure in English life was now a respectable bourgeois, who had no desire to make himself conspicuous but wished merely to present a gentlemanly appearance, both in his counting-house and at home. The author we have already quoted recommends dark blue or black for town wear, although he allows a tweed suit to be worn in the country. What we are watching, in fact,

in this period is the fading away of flamboyance and colour from men's garments, not to be recovered until very modern times. It was considered ungentlemanly to wear anything striking.

Ill. 190

The same was true of women; quietness and delicacy were the qualities most admired. Indeed, it was fashionable to be, or to appear, a little *souffrante*; 'rude health' was positively vulgar. Rouge was entirely abandoned, 'interesting pallor' was admired, and some foolish young women even went so far as to drink vinegar in order to conform to the prevailing fashion. The prosperous businessman, who had now begun to desert the city and to establish his family in a fine new house in the fashionable suburbs, asked two things of his wife: first that she should be a model of domestic virtues and second that she should not do anything at all. Her complete idleness was the mark of his social status. Work of any kind was looked down on, and the clothes which reflected this attitude were of an

190 *Convalescence*, after
Eugène Lami, *c.* 1845

191 Day dresses, from *Le Follet*,
c. 1848. Examples of the extremely
modest styles of the 1840s. The
Queen's passion for Balmoral
encouraged the use of Scotch
plaids

extremely restrictive kind. Indeed, the large number of petti-coats worn at this period prevented women from pursuing any activities without fatigue.

This seems all the more strange when we consider that in the world outside the home the 1840s was a decade of quite extraordinary innovation and upheaval. It saw the introduction of railways; it also witnessed a series of social upheavals cul-minating in 1848, the Year of Revolutions. In all this, women were supposed to have no part, and the vast majority of women seem to have accepted this situation with meekness and resig-nation. Prudery reigned supreme; skirts were now down to the ground, and the little feet in flat-heeled slippers could barely be glimpsed beneath the underskirts. As sensible a writer as Thackeray thinks it necessary to apologize for mentioning ankles. There never was a period when women, with the exception of the straight-across décolleté in the evening, were more completely covered up. The poke bonnet prevented even their faces from being seen except from directly in front.

Such a state of affairs did not, naturally, suit all women, and, in France at least, there was a wave of rebellion, symbolized by the figure of the *lionne*. A contemporary writer defines the *lionne* as a 'rich married woman, pretty and coquettish, who can handle the whip and the pistol as well as her husband, ride like a lancer, smoke like a dragoon, and drink any quantity of iced champagne'. 'Ride like a lancer' is the operative phrase. There was a passion for horsemanship among women in the early 1840s, and all fashionable magazines of the period show riding costume. The curious point about it is that it is masculin-ized down to the waist but no further. The practical thing, of course, would have been to masculinize the nether limbs; but it was unthinkable at this period that women should wear bifurcated garments, and they always rode side-saddle. Work-ing from the head to the feet, we may note that the correct female riding habit consisted of a man's top hat with a veil rather loosely attached to it, a man's collar and tie, a man's coat and waistcoat and an extremely voluminous skirt. In fact the

192 Winter dress, 1847

skirt was so voluminous that it reached almost to the ground when the wearer was in the saddle (as can be seen quite plainly in the equestrian statues of Queen Victoria at this period) and made it almost impossible to alight from the horse without help from a groom. The unconscious motivation is plain enough. One of the purposes of dress is (or perhaps we should say was) to show that the wearer is of high social status and can afford to employ a retinue of servants.

The essential lines of female costume during the 1840s may be briefly summarized. The waist was low, and the lines of decoration on the bodice were designed to make it look even more so. The sleeves were either tight or had a bulge over the lower arm; the skirts were long and full. Bodice and skirt were usually made in one, with a back fastening by means of hooks and eyes, but from the middle of the decade it was possible to have a jacket bodice separate from the skirt. The jacket bodice was close-fitting and buttoned down the front. There was also a garment known as a *gilet-cuirasse* which looked like a man's waistcoat and was sometimes a separate garment and sometimes joined to the jacket. Skirts were made to stand out by lining, and sometimes there was an additional woollen inter-lining added to the upper part of the skirt at the back. Many petticoats were worn, and what might be described as the tea-cosy effect was further emphasized by the use of a small bustle made of horsehair. This, to the confusion of modern students, was known as a 'crinoline'. It was quite different from the crino-line of the future, but etymologically the term was more correct than when it was applied to the steel hoops of the 1850s and 1860s, for *crin* is the French for 'horsehair', and that was the substance of which the early 'crinolines' was made. Skirts were nearly always adorned with flounces, which might be double or multiple, or else with ruching and other decoration.

Scholars distinguish four types of day dresses – the pelisse-robe, the redingote, the round dress and the peignoir – but there was a considerable amount of confusion and overlapping, and by the end of the decade the first two terms were used indiscriminately. In general it may be said that the pelisse-robe was worn indoors in the morning, the redingote was used for the 'promenade', and the rather more decorated round dress was worn in the afternoon. The peignoir was an informal dress worn only in the morning, but it was not in the modern sense of the word a dressing-gown.

Evening dresses were décolleté, off the shoulder and either straight across or with a slight dip in the middle. The term for the latter was *en cœur*. The horizontal pleats across the top of the corsage are very typical of this period, as was also the deep 'bertha' which fell from the top of the corsage to halfway down the sleeves and was made up of lace and frills or ribbon. The body of the bodice came to a point in front and was strongly boned. The favourite materials for day dresses were broadcloth, merino, foulard, organdie, gingham and tarlatan. Evening dresses were usually made of shot silk or velvet.

174

Outdoor garments were of various types. The shawl had now come back into favour and was sometimes very large with a fringed border. Paisley shawls were no longer considered a mere substitute for imported cashmere, for the Queen's residence at Balmoral had brought all things Scottish into favour. Various new forms of the cloak were invented, and were given different names according to whether they had capes, sleeves or slits through the arms or all three together. The differences between casawecks, polkas and pardessus were trifling; the names are a reminder of the influence at this time of some of the costumes of Eastern Europe, particularly those of Hungary.

Everything was done at this period to make women look as small as possible, partly perhaps in deference to Queen Victoria, who was of diminutive stature. Footwear, with rare exceptions, was therefore made without heels. The usual form was the slipper, sometimes laced over the ankles like that of a ballerina but without the reinforced toe. Such slippers were made of silk or crêpe in colours matching the dress. Very small feet were admired as a mark of gentility. In the street it was customary to wear cloth boots with elastic sides, but genteel ladies did not venture much abroad. By 1850, mid-Victorian modes, for men and women, seemed to have set in a mould. Those who wore them saw no reason why they should ever change.

Mantles for the theatre, 1835

LE FOLLET

193 Day dresses, 1853. The skirt with many flounces is very typical of the early 1850s. Its shape is maintained by a multiplicity of petticoats, the crinoline not yet having béen brought in to support it

CHAPTER EIGHT

From 1850 to 1900

AFTER the Hungry Forties, the bustling, prosperous Fifties. The Year of Revolutions (1848) had resulted in the defeat of the Left all over Europe. In some countries this had resulted in the re-establishment of centralized tyranny; but in England and France it was really the triumph of the *bourgeoisie*. It is true that the *coup d'état* of Louis Napoleon in 1851 gave rise to some anxiety, but in spite of his military adventures later in the decade, the real supporters of Napoleon III were the bankers, industrialists and capitalists. In England the Great Exhibition of 1851 not only demonstrated new kinds of technology but gave hope (a misguided hope as it turned out) that an era of universal peace and brotherhood was about to begin. Trade and commerce were certainly flourishing. We have only to look at the immense number of houses in London with stucco fronts and a portico with two pillars, nearly all of them built in the 1850s, to realize that the London businessman and merchant now had enough money to cease living 'over the shop' in the City and retire to the gentility of South Kensington and Belgravia.

Increasing prosperity meant an increasing elaboration of dress, and we find R. S. Surtees, in one of his novels (*Ask Mamma*, 1853), complaining that 'the housemaid now dresses better – finer at all events – than her mistress did twenty years ago, and it is almost impossible to recognize working people when they are in their Sunday dresses'. Skirts continued to expand, and for the first half of the decade the desired effect was obtained by wearing underneath them a larger number of petticoats. The weight of these finally became intolerable, and in 1856 they were replaced by a 'cage crinoline' or hooped petticoat.

194 *A Windy Corner*, 1864. The crinoline is now worn by every woman, and even by the little girl pushing the primitive perambulator

This was not, of course, the first time that skirts had been supported by hoops. We have already noted the clumsy cartwheel farthingale of the Elizabethan period and the side panniers of the eighteenth century, but the new crinoline was a much more scientific apparatus, for technology was now sufficiently advanced for the manufacturers to be able to supply *Ill. 196* flexible steel hoops which could either form a separate garment, hung by tapes from the waist, or be sewn into a petticoat.

When the crinoline was first invented, it must have seemed to women an instrument of liberation. No longer hampered by multiple layers of petticoat, they could, inside their steel cage, move their limbs freely. Of course there was a danger in this, and the caricaturists of the period delighted to show what could happen to crinolined ladies 'in a high wind'. Legs were still supposed to be invisible, and in case of mischance it was customary to wear long linen pantaloons edged with lace and sometimes reaching to the ankle. Little girls also wore *Ill. 195* these pantaloons in spite of the fact that their skirts were comparatively short. Indeed, it became a mark of gentility for the lace pantaloons to be seen. Mothers who could not afford the

178

complete garment had to be content with what were called 'pantalettes', which were simply tubes of white linen ending just above the knee. These strange compromise garments were sold in enormous numbers.

It seems to be one of the principles of fashion that once an exaggeration has been decided on it becomes ever more exaggerated. Thus, by the end of the decade, the crinoline-supported skirts were truly prodigious, until it was impossible for two women to enter the room together or sit on the same sofa, for the frills of one dress took up all available space. A woman was now a majestic ship, sailing proudly ahead, while a small tender – her male escort – sailed along behind.

195 Girls in crinoline dresses and pantaloons, 1853

196 Crinoline petticoat, c. 1860. The crinoline is circular in form and consists of eight hoops of flexible steel wire

All this did not pass without protest. Even before the crinoline had come into being there were rumours from America of a new movement for a rational dress for women. The formidable *Ill. 199* Mrs Bloomer came to England in 1851 to spread her gospel and to try to induce women to adopt her sensible and certainly not unfeminine costume. This consisted of a simplified version of the bodice in vogue, and a fairly ample skirt which reached well below the knee. Underneath it, however, were to be seen baggy trousers reaching to the ankle, usually with a lace frill at the bottom. This very modest attempt to reform female dress provoked an almost unbelievable outburst of excitement,

197 Paris fashions for September 1859

198 *In a box at the Opera*, from *Le Follet*, 1857. The woman who is not décolleté is presumably a maid or theatre attendant

199 Mrs Amelia Bloomer, *c.* 1850. Mrs Bloomer's very modest attempts to reform female dress met with a storm of hostility and ridicule

200 Right, *Une tournure à faire tourner toutes les têtes!*, by Charles Vernier. The silhouette of male and female costume has never differed more drastically than in 1860

ridicule and vituperation. What might be called the trouser complex came into full play. Women were endeavouring, it seemed, to 'wear the trousers', and the mid-Victorian man regarded this as an outrageous attack on his own privileged position. *Punch*, that faithful mirror of middle-class opinion in the nineteenth century, brought out dozens of cartoons emphasizing the consequences of a possible sexual revolution, a world in which timid men were in complete subjection to their bloomered spouses.

As the husband, shall the wife be; he will have to wear a gown
If he does not quickly make her put her Bloomer short-coats down.

However, as an attempt to influence contemporary fashion, the Bloomer Movement was a complete failure. A few 'advanced' ladies adopted the costume, but the upper classes refused to have anything to do with it, and Mrs Bloomer had to wait for almost fifty years before she had her revenge in the adoption of 'bloomers' for cycling.

Her attempt was premature, for the mid-nineteenth century was the high-water mark of male domination, and in such patriarchal periods the clothes of the two sexes are as clearly differentiated as possible. A visitor from Mars contemplating a man in frock coat and top hat and a woman in a crinoline might well have supposed that they belonged to different species. And the crinoline certainly bore a symbolic relation to the age in which it thrived. In one of its aspects it symbolized female fertility, as an expansion of the apparent size of the hips always seems to do. This was an age of big families, and since the rate of infant mortality was not quite so high as it had been in previous periods, the population of England expanded rapidly.

In another sense the crinoline was a symbol of the supposed unapproachability of women. The expanded skirt seemed to say: 'You cannot come near enough to me even to kiss my hand.' But of course the enormously expanded skirt was a hollow sham; it was itself an instrument of seduction. As I have written elsewhere, 'when we see engravings of ladies with skirts like old-fashioned tea-cosies we are apt to think of the structure as solid and immovable; but, of course, nothing was further from the truth. The crinoline was in a constant state of *Ill. 200* agitation, thrown from side to side. It was like a rather restless captive balloon, and not at all, except in shape, like the igloo of the Eskimos. It swayed now to one side, now to the other, tipped up a little, swung forward and backward. Any pressure on one side of the steel hoops was communicated by their elasticity to the other side, and resulted in a certain upward shooting of the skirt. It was probably this upward shooting which gave mid-Victorian men their complex about ankles, and it certainly resulted in a new fashion in boots' (*Taste and Fashion*). Throughout the Forties the footwear of women had been reduced to a heelless slipper, scarcely seen among the voluminousness of the dress; but now boots came in, with higher heels and laced half-way up towards the calf. The crinoline was certainly not a moral garment, and the period in

184

201 *The Empress Eugénie and her maids of honour*, by F. X. Winterhalter, *c.* 1860

which it reached its greatest development, Second Empire France, was not a moral period. The social history of the Second Empire is the history of the *grande cocotte*.

There certainly seems to have been a symbolic relationship between the crinoline and the Second Empire, with its material prosperity, its extravagance, its expansionist tendencies – and its hypocrisy. And the Queen of the Crinoline was the Empress Eugénie herself. She was perhaps the last Royal personage to *Ill. 201* have a direct and immediate influence on fashion, and the crinoline suited her style to perfection. It was never more proudly or effectively displayed than during her reign. And now a new race of fashion designers had arisen to transform the whole world of *haute couture*.

202 Crinoline dress by
Worth, *c.* 1860. As
Worth could not draw,
he had lithographs
made of heads and
arms and then sketched
in the dress

In former ages the fashion designer had been a comparatively humble person, visiting ladies in their homes. And the vast majority of them had been women. Now M. Worth, who, in spite of being an Englishman, had in ten years made himself a dictator of the mode in Paris, required ladies (with the exception of Eugénie and her Court) to come to *him*. The French historian Hippolyte Taine has described the scene, as ladies, anxious to be dressed by Worth, waited upon him in his salon.

'This little dry, black, nervous creature sees them in a velvet coat, carelessly stretched out on a divan, a cigar between his lips. He says to them, "Walk! turn! good! come back in a week, and I will compose you a toilette which will suit you." It is not they who choose it, it is he. They are only too happy to let him do it, and even for that need an introduction. Mme B., a personage of the *Beau Monde* and elegant to boot, went to him last month to order a dress. "Madame", he said, "By whom are you presented?" "I don't understand." "I'm afraid you must be presented in order to be dressed by me."

186

203 London and Paris fashions for June 1864. The crinoline has begun to slip to the back and is no longer a perfect circle

She went away, suffocated with rage. But others stayed, saying, "I don't care how rude he is so long as he dresses me." ' Worth soon had innumerable imitators, but few or none equalled his *panache* or his success.

The crinoline lasted for about fifteen years and in that time went through several modifications. It reached its greatest extent about the year 1860. At that time it projected as much to the front as to the back. The skirt looked like a bee-hive, not only from the front but from the side. Waists were tight, and the bodice was fitted to the figure; but out of doors it was the custom to wear a shawl or mantalette, with the result that a woman's general appearance was that of a broad-based triangle, the effect being enhanced by the smallness of the bonnet, which had now begun to slip back from the forehead to reveal the front hair. Then, in the mid 1860s, the crinoline began to slip *Ill. 203* to the back of the skirt, leaving the front more or less straight, and in 1868 there was a further change, the reinforcement of the skirt having slipped entirely to the back and being indeed no more than a half-crinoline. There was a mass of material at the back, ending in a train, and when the crinoline was removed altogether, towards the end of the Sixties, this was looped up into a kind of bustle, the characteristic of the next decade. The crinoline, in fact, having served as a symbol of the Second Empire, collapsed with it like a pricked balloon. In the street it was the fashion for younger women to wear a shorter skirt, which could be looped up by means of strings to reveal a skirt underneath, but this was a very temporary fashion, the skirts of the Seventies being excessively long and trailing.

The defeat of France in 1870 and the troubles of the following year kept Paris out of the picture for a while, and it was some time before she recovered her ascendancy. Contemporary writers saw a return to a greater simplicity, though to our eyes the dresses of the early 1870s seem voluminous and luxurious enough. They even seem a little garish, an effect to which two recent inventions contributed. One was the sewing machine, and the other the introduction of aniline dyes. Gone were the

204 *Women in the garden*, by Claude Monet, 1866–7. Even in light
summer dresses the crinoline was still considered essential

subdued soft colours of the former decade, their place being taken by all kinds of bright hues. It was the fashion to have the bodice of a different colour from the skirt and to cut the dress out of two different materials, one patterned and one plain, the plain portion of the dress being trimmed with the patterned material and the patterned portion being trimmed with the plain. The effect was sometimes that of a patchwork quilt, and a writer in the magazine *The Young Englishwoman* (1876) complains that 'it is now impossible to describe dresses with exactitude: the skirts are draped so mysteriously, the arrangements of trimmings is usually one-sided and the fastenings are so curiously contrived that if I study any particular toilette for even a quarter of an hour the task of writing down how it is all made remains hopeless.'

LE JOURNAL DES MODES.

205 Left, London and Paris fashions for March 1869. The silhouette is now straight down the front and the crinoline is about to give place to the bustle

206 Headdresses, 1870

Bonnets had now given way to hats, very small hats perched over the forehead and worn on top of a mass of hair which now formed an enormous chignon of plaits or curls. So much hair was required for this new fashion that many women were unable to provide it themselves, and enormous quantities of hair was imported and made up into 'scalpettes' and 'frizzettes'. Seen from the side, the shape of the back of the hair was a curious echo of the shape of the back of the skirt.

Ill. 206

Ill. 207

The dresses were of two kinds: those which were all in one piece (the·so-called 'Princess' style) and those which consisted of a separate bodice and skirt. The jacket bodice was carried over from the previous decade and was made with short basques or with long basques forming a kind of overskirt. A loose skirt in a contrasting material or colour was sometimes worn with this garment; and a similar effect was obtained from the cuirasse bodice, which came in about 1874 and often had a plastron of different material down the front. The cuirasse bodice was very tight and moulded to the hips. This necessitated the use of a long, tight corset, and ladies who did not wish to encase themselves in this in the home wore a blouse. Sleeves were in general tight. An overskirt was sometimes used; it was draped at the sides in various ways, and in the early 1870s was, as we have seen, bunched out at the back into a bustle.

El David Dias Paris   *Imp Lemercier & C.ᵢᵉ r de Seine Sᵗ Paris*

The Duke of Edinburgh.   The Grand Duchess Marie Alexandróvna.

207 Fashion plate from the *Tailor and Cutter, c.* 1870. A curious example of the practice at this period of sticking the heads of well-known people on a fashion plate

208 Lady's and child's dresses, September 1873, from the *Journal des Demoiselles*

The 'Princess' style was capable of considerable variety, one of the most popular of which was the polonaise, sometimes buttoned all down the front. The popularity of Dickens's *Barnaby Rudge* brought in the 'Dolly Varden' dress. It was usually of brightly patterned chintz or cretonne, and was fondly imagined by its wearers to be some kind of eighteenth-century costume. It was worn with a picture hat tilted forward over the forehead. At the end of the decade a knitted costume came in. It was made fashionable by Mrs Langtry, the 'Jersey Lily', and was therefore known as the 'jersey dress'. Another variety was the tea gown, which was loose enough to allow corsets to be discarded. Originally intended as a *robe de chambre* – and the name indicates its French origin – it had become very elaborate by the late 1870s, with many frills and flounces and much lace. *Ill. 208* It was essentially a matron's gown, and a lace cap was always worn with it.

209 *Madame Moitessier*, by J.-A.-D. Ingres, 1844/5–56

210 *Derby Day*, by
William Powell Frith,
1856–8

211 *Omnibus Life
in London*, by
William Egley,
1859. In the
mid-century the
crinoline was still
in full swing in
spite of the
inconvenience of
squeezing it into
the narrow
confines of an
omnibus

212 Ladies' and
child's costume,
March 1877

Journal des Demoiselles

Ills. 212,
213

By the middle of the decade the bunched-up bustle had disappeared. The skirts were still full at the back, but the fullness was lower down, and even day dresses were provided with a surprisingly long train – to the disgust of Ruskin and others, who pointed out how very unhygienic such a style must necessarily be. Skirts were extremely hampering and, about 1876, we find in *Punch* a whole series of cartoons depicting ladies whose dress was so tight that they could neither sit down nor climb stairs. The waist was ferociously tight-laced, and it was made to look even smaller by wearing the corset, so to speak, outside, as part of the bodice running down to a sharp

213 Evening dresses, c. 1877

point in front. This became the prevailing mode in the early 1880s, the skirt emerging underneath the corset bodice being horizontally draped to make the waist look smaller still. In the mid 1880s there was a revival of the bustle, but it was of a different kind. It stuck out horizontally from the small of the back, but the supporting structure was no longer, as it had been in the early 1870s, a contrivance of horsehair. We find advertisements of 'the braided wire health bustle, warranted to be less heating to the spine than any others'. There was also the 'Langtry' bustle, an arrangement of metal bands working on a pivot. It could be raised when sitting down and sprang back automatically into place when the lady rose to her feet! One of the most extraordinary inventions in the whole history of fashion.

Ills. 214–15

Ill. 218

214 Left, *Too Early*, by
James Tissot, 1873. The
gentleman in the
doorway has brought
his 'gibus' (crush hat)
into the ballroom, as
was the custom

215 *La Grande Jatte*, by
Georges Seurat, 1884–6.
The bustle of the
mid 1880s is quite
different from the
bustle of the 1870s

216 Evening and
visiting dress, 1884. The
extreme form of the
second bustle built over
a wire frame

One cannot omit from a study of the 1880s some reference to
Ill. 217 Aesthetic costume, and to the Rational Dress movement. Some
intellectuals, as a protest against the ugliness of contemporary
fashion, began to wear clothes influenced by those of the Pre-
Raphaelites. In essentials they followed the lines of fashion but
were looser, with full sleeves, and were worn with no corset,
heel-less shoes and softer, less formally arranged hair-styles.
Punch satirized these clothes, particularly male Aesthetic dress:
knee-breeches, a velvet jacket, a flowing tie and wideawake
hat. This was the costume worn by Oscar Wilde, who was
associated with the Aesthetes and the Rational Dress movement, on his lecture tour of America, and also by Bunthorne
in Gilbert and Sullivan's *Patience*, which made the whole
Aesthetic movement the target of its ridicule. Members of the
Rational Dress movement, which originated in 1881, were
concerned about the unhealthiness of current fashion, protesting
particularly about the tight and deforming corset and about
unnecessary layers of clothes, padding and boning. Although
scorned by many at the time, the movement did eventually
achieve its aims, as women began to lead more active lives and
rigid corsets thus became unfashionable.

217 *Nincompoopiana – The Mutual Admiration Society*, by George du
Maurier, 1880. Satire on the costumes and attitudes of the Aesthetes

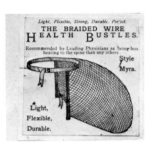

218 Bustle advertisements. The horsehair bustles of the 1870s and the 'scientific' bustles of the 1880s. The 'Health Bustle' is recommended as being 'less heating to the spine than any others'. The 'Langtry' bustle folded up to allow the wearer to sit down and sprang into place again when she got up

219 *The Reception*, by James Tissot, 1886. No nineteenth-century painter is more useful to the costume historian than Tissot. He observed the *toilettes* of the period with the greatest attention and painted them with meticulous accuracy

220 *The Picnic*, by James Tissot, 1875. Informal clothes, painted in the garden of Tissot's own house in St John's Wood

Ordinary male costume at this period showed little change from that of the preceding decade. The cut-away coat was worn only in the evening and was embellished with black silk facings. For daytime the frock coat had now established itself as the accepted town wear. Another possibility was the morning coat, cut away in a curve over the hips and buttoning rather high over the chest. Among the young, the short jacket was becoming increasingly popular, particularly at Oxford and Cambridge. Double-breasted 'reefer' jackets were also worn, especially for yachting. The influence of sport is very noticeable at this period. All kinds of new sports were now coming into favour, and it was impossible to practise them with any comfort in the formal dress of the day. For shooting, a man could wear a Norfolk jacket, with its characteristic belt and vertical pleats,

221 *Les Parapluies*, by Renoir, *c.* 1884. Renoir is a very useful portrayer of ordinary middle- and working-class costume at this period

and rather loose knee-breeches with gaiters. The hat worn with this outfit was of soft felt and sometimes had a dent in the crown like the later homburg. Cricket costume was the same as today, except that it was still permissible to wear a coloured shirt. Bright-coloured blazers were now coming into fashion.

Ill. 222 For the new sport of cycling, which was still in the 'penny-farthing' stage, an extraordinary costume was devised: tight-fitting knee-breeches, a very tight, military-looking jacket and a little pillbox cap. The really smart wearer of this outfit carried a bugle to warn pedestrians of his approach. This peculiar get-up does not seem to have been adopted in France and Germany, where cycling was almost equally popular.

222 Male and female cycling costume, 1878–80

223 Male and female seaside costume, 1886

THE MILITARY.   THE PRINCESS.   CHESTERFIELD.   THE LOUNGE.

224 British spring and summer costume, 1884

The most popular overcoat was the chesterfield, which began *Ill. 224* by being knee-length but gradually grew longer; it was made of such materials as miltons, worsteds and cheviots, in black, brown, blue or grey. It usually had silk facings and was edged with braid. The top frock was almost a replica of the frock coat underneath, except, of course, that it was cut more loosely and was generally made of heavier material. The inverness and the ulster were capes, or rather half-capes, attached to a coat. A short double-breasted overcoat, with a shoulder cape sometimes trimmed with fur, was called the 'Gladstone' overcoat; another variety with a half-circle cape was known as the 'Albert'. In the evening the tail coat was still essential at all formal functions, but the dinner jacket was increasingly worn at home or when dining at the club. When the ladies had retired, it was permitted

205

to put on a smoking jacket. This was similar in form to the dinner jacket, but was almost invariably quilted, presumably for warmth, since the smoking rooms and billiard rooms of country houses were often unheated.

There is little difference between male costume in the 1880s and in the 1890s, except for the increasing use of informal attire. It was still considered rather 'caddish' to wear anything but a frock coat or a morning coat in town, when paying calls or when taking part in the Sunday church parade in Hyde Park. Lounge suits could be of blue serge or patterned tweeds. With them it was quite permissible to wear a fancy waistcoat, sometimes extremely brightly patterned, although the *Tailor and Cutter* issued a warning in 1890 that 'gentlemen with abdominal convexity will use discretion in the employment of hues and patterns calculated to draw attention to that unromantic formation'. Trousers in the early 1890s were of the peg-top variety, and dashing young men began to wear them with turn-ups. These, however, were still looked on with disfavour, and it created quite a sensation when, in 1893, Viscount Lewisham appeared in the House of Commons wearing them.

Ties and bows could be adjusted in several ways. Sometimes they were ready-made. The height of the collar increased steadily throughout the decade until it became a real 'choker'.

The bustle finally disappeared from female costume, together with the horizontal skirt draperies so characteristic of the 1880s. Dresses were smooth over the hips and made to fit more snugly by being cut on the cross. Skirts were long and bell-shaped and usually had a train even when worn in the street. Day dresses were high in the neck and finished with ruching or a large bow of tulle. A good deal of lace was worn, even day blouses being elaborately adorned. Some evening gowns were made entirely of lace, and much was worn also on petticoats, which now assumed a new importance. Since it was impossible to cross the street without holding up the long skirt with one hand, the gesture inevitably displayed the lace frilling of the petticoat, which seems to have had at this period an

225 *Portrait of Sonja Knips*, by Gustav Klimt, 1898

extraordinary amount of erotic appeal. Sleeves, which at the beginning of the decade were peaked at the shoulders but otherwise fairly narrow, had grown to enormous proportions *Ill. 229* by 1894. Some sleeves were so large that cushions were necessary to keep them in place. They were even thought essential in stage costume and fancy dress – a requirement which, on the stage, made any attempt at historical accuracy in period plays an impossibility.

By now, the bicycle had become immensely popular. This made it inevitable that some kind of bifurcated garment should be worn, since it was impossible to ride a bicycle in a trailing *Ill. 226* skirt. Divided skirts were one solution and so were baggy knickerbockers called 'bloomers'. They caused almost as much excitement as the original bloomer campaign of the 1850s. They were ridiculed in the Press and denounced in the pulpit, but it was all to no avail; young women continued to wear them. Indeed, the new enthusiasm for outdoor sports of all kinds made it necessary to wear more rational garments in general and there was a new vogue for the tailored suit, consisting of jacket, skirt and 'shirtwaister'. The odd thing is that

226 Cycling dress, March 1894

227, 228 Left, in the garden, 1891. Right, riding costume, February 1894

when women went in for outdoor pursuits they insisted on wearing men's hats and men's stiff white collars. Sports clothes *Ill. 228* for women were in general heavy, made of homespuns or tweeds, and the colours were usually dark.

Hats throughout the decade were rather small and perched squarely on the top of the head. Outdoor garments consisted of mantles, cloaks and capes, the first two terms being more or less interchangeable. The cape, however, was usually shorter, fitted closely over the shoulders and reached to the waist. The early mantles often had medici collars up to the ears, kept in position by means of wires. Many women wore the masculine chesterfields and three-quarter-length coats. Shoes had comparatively high heels and rounded toes and were laced up the front. Boots could be laced or buttoned. They were made of leather or cloth. Stockings were nearly always black, of lisle

229 Autumn walking dress, 1895   230 At the races, 1894
Examples of the extreme form of the balloon sleeve in the mid 1890s

thread in the daytime and silk in the evening. In the evening
it was fashionable to wear very long suede gloves, sometimes
with as many as twenty buttons, and to carry a very large fan
of curved or straight ostrich feathers. Jewellery was extensively
Ill. 232 worn. Colours in general were rather bright and discordant,
the favourite of all being yellow. It is no accident that the
most exciting publication of the decade was called *The Yellow
Book*.

Political events were not without their effect on fashion.
The dominance of Paris was still unquestioned, and the French
Government was now inclined to ally itself with Russia. The
Russian fleet visited Toulon in 1893, and three years later the
Tsar himself came to Paris amid scenes of the greatest en-
thusiasm. This inaugurated a vogue for furs, which were

210

231 Travelling costume, 1898   232 Walking dress, February 1899

adopted by women as well as by men: in former ages fur had been almost entirely a male prerogative. The position was now somewhat reversed, in that women wore furs in the form not only of trimmings, but of whole fur coats, whereas men's fur coats had the fur on the inside, the fur being visible only in the collar and the cuffs.

The 1890s as a whole was a period of changing values. The old, rigid society-mould was visibly breaking up, with South African millionaires and other *nouveaux riches* storming the citadels of the aristocracy. For the young there was a new breath of freedom in the air, symbolized both by their sports costumes and by the extravagance of their ordinary dress. It was perfectly plain that the Victorian Age was drawing to its close.

211

233 *The Wertheimer Sisters*, by John Singer Sargent, *c.* 1901

CHAPTER NINE

From 1900 to 1939

THE PERIOD from the beginning of the century to the outbreak of World War I is usually spoken of in England as the Edwardian era, although the King actually died in 1910. In France, with a slight extension backwards into the middle of the 1890s, it was referred to as *la belle époque*. In both countries the atmosphere was very similar. It was an age of great ostentation and extravagance. In England, society and the Court, which had of course always overlapped, now began to coincide and the King himself set the example. As Virginia Cowles remarks, 'The fact that the King liked City men, millionaires, Jewish jokes and American heiresses and pretty women (regardless of their origin) meant that the doors were open to anyone who succeeded in titillating the Monarch's fancy. . . . Edwardian society modelled itself to suit the King's personal demands. Everything was larger than lifesize. There was an avalanche of balls and dinners and country house parties. More money was spent on clothes, more food was consumed, more horses were raced, more infidelities were committed, more birds were shot, more yachts were commissioned, more late hours were kept, than ever before' (*Edward VII and His Circle*, London 1956).

Fashion as always reflected the age. Like the King himself it favoured the mature woman, cool and commanding with a rather heavy bust, the effect of which was further emphasized by the so-called 'health' corsets which, in a laudable effort to prevent a downward pressure on the abdomen, made the body rigidly straight in front by throwing forward the bust and throwing back the hips. This produced the peculiar S-shaped stance so characteristic of the period. The skirt, smooth over the hips, flared out towards the ground in the shape of a bell.

234 Evening dress: *Il a-été primé*. Fashion plate from the *Gazette du Bon Ton*, 1914

235 Evening gowns by Paul Poiret. Cover of *Art-Goût-Beauté*, March 1923

Créations
PAUL POIRET

Cascades of lace descended from the corsage; indeed there was a passion for lace in every part of the gown. For those who could not afford real lace there was a considerable vogue for Irish crochet. The hair was built high on the head, and the flat pancake hat projected forward as if to balance the train. In the evening the dresses were extravagantly décolleté, but in the daytime the whole body was concealed from the ears to the feet. The little lace collar was kept in place by boning, and the arms were always completely concealed by long gloves. There was a rage for feathers, hats being adorned with one or more plumes; feather boas were worn round the neck. The best examples were made entirely of ostrich plumes and sometimes cost as much as ten guineas.

216

236, 237 Left, spring dresses
trimmed with silk braid and with
lace, May 1900

238 Straight-fronted corset,
February 1902

239 Chiffon dress, 1901

240 Evening dress, September 1901

241 Summer dress, c. 1903

242 Silk evening dress, 1911

243 Evening dress with lace, 1907–8

Photographs of the actual dresses, showing the texture of the materials

218

244 So-called 'Merveilleuse' dresses produced a sensation at the Longchamps races in May 1908. It was a strange delusion that these dresses resembled in any way the flimsy 'Empire' costumes of the 1790s

245 Dress of 1908. The period of the 'Gibson Girl', with heavy bust and swirling skirt, created by the artist Charles Dana Gibson. She was based on the beautiful Langhorne sisters, one of whom Gibson married

One sometimes wonders if the climate of Europe was very much better in the early years of the century than it has been since: so many of the clothes of the period look as if they had been designed for a garden party or to be worn at a Riviera casino. In the winter the greater part of smart society seems to have swarmed over to Monte Carlo and similar Mediterranean resorts. Whatever the ups and downs of the *entente* in political circles, it was plain that the English upper classes, once more following the example of the King, regarded France and England as parts of the same civilization, stamping grounds for the same round of pleasure. The period has been defined as 'the last good time of the upper classes', and even the colours of clothes reflected the sunny optimism of those that had money to spend. It was all pastel shades of pink, pale blue or mauve, or black with small sequins sewn all over it. The favourite materials were crêpe de chine, chiffon, *mousseline de soie* and tulle. Many satin dresses were embroidered in floral patterns with little clusters of ribbon, or even painted by hand. The amount of sheer labour which went into the making of one fashionable gown was truly prodigious; one would have to go back to the embroidered brocades of the early eighteenth century to find anything comparable.

The blouse had now become an extremely elaborate confection. It was adorned with tucking and insertion. 'Some blouses', says a writer in a contemporary fashion magazine, 'have circular trimmings of fluted muslin, giving a pretty graceful curve, and the trimming has a very fussy look.' The bolero was extremely popular, as was also the so-called Eton bodice, a garment like a boy's Eton jacket. The balloon sleeves of the 1890s had now been completely abandoned, sleeves in general being tight at the wrist and rather long so as to extend half over the hand. The tea gown, once merely a means of 'getting into something loose', was now an artistic creation in its own right.

Another feature of this period, however, is the importance of tailor-mades. A considerable number of young women of

246 Lady's golfing costume, 1907   247 Day dress, 1907

the middle classes were now beginning to earn their living as governesses, typists and shop assistants, and it would have been impossible for them to pursue their occupations in the elaborate garden-party dresses we have been describing. Even rich women wore tailor-mades in the country or when travel- *Ills. 246–7* ling, and the English tailors, rightly reputed to be the best in the world, reaped a rich harvest.

For men the accepted wear for all formal occasions was still the top hat and the frock coat, but the lounge suit worn with a homburg hat (a name derived from the German spa, much visited by the Prince of Wales) was increasingly to be seen, even in the West End of London. Straw hats were extremely popular and were sometimes worn even with riding breeches; trousers tended to be rather short and very narrow, and young men were beginning to wear them with permanent turn-ups and with a sharp crease in front, which had become possible since the mid 1890s with the invention of the trouser-press. Collars of white starched linen were extremely high and sometimes went right round the throat. This was an echo, as it were, of the boned necks of female attire.

Ill. 244   The female silhouette began to be slightly modified in 1908. The bust was no longer thrust quite so far forward, nor the hips so far back. Floppy blouses hanging over the waist in front were abandoned. The fashionable 'Empire' gown, although bearing very little resemblance to the dresses worn in the time of Napoleon I, had the effect of narrowing the hips. This can be seen quite plainly in the corset advertisements of the period. Hats became wider, which had the effect of making the hips look narrower still.

248 Far left, male summer costume, July 1907

249 Left, walking dress, 1910

250 Right, lady's motoring costume, April 1905. In the open motor-cars of the period it was necessary to be protected from cold and, above all, from dust

251 Flannel suit for boating, July 1902

252 Male motoring costume, c. 1904

And then, in 1910, there was a fundamental change in female dress. There has been much argument as to what brought this about, but it was plain that the Russian Ballet had something *Ills. 257–9* to do with it, and so had Paul Poiret, and we need not trouble ourselves with the question of which came first. What is certain is that there was a wave of Orientalism following the extraordinary excitement caused by the production of *Schéhérazade*, the costumes for which were designed by Leon Bakst. The colours were striking, even garish, and society adopted them with enthusiasm. The old pale pinks and 'swooning mauves' were swept away; the rigid bodices and bell-shaped skirts were abandoned in favour of soft drapery. Skirts became narrow at the hem, and in 1910 extremely so, *Ill. 253* resulting in the hobble skirt which made it difficult for a woman to take a step of more than two or three inches. To prevent women from taking a longer stride and so splitting the skirt, a fetter made of braid was sometimes worn. It was as if every woman – and this in the very year of the Suffragette demonstrations – was determined to look like a slave in an Oriental harem. Some women even went so far as to wear little 'harem'

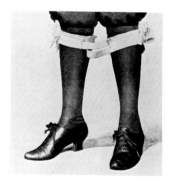

253, 254 Emancipated woman: Hobble-skirt dresses and hobble garter, 1910

255, 256 The new silhouette, still heavy above but tapering towards the feet, seen at race meetings in 1914

trousers visible below the hem of the skirt, but these created such a sensation when worn in the street that only the most daring persisted. With the extremely narrow skirt went very large hats. The silhouette, in complete contrast to that of the woman of 1860, was a triangle standing on its point. The favourite trimming of dresses was no longer lace but buttons, which were sewn all over, even in the most unlikely places.

Designers prospered. Lucile (Lady Duff-Gordon), who had made her mark by designing Lily Elsie's costume for *The Merry Widow* in 1907, was, like Poiret, working on a romantic Oriental theme. She, and Charles Creed and Redfern, famous for their tailor-mades derived from men's suits, all established branches in Paris at this time.

258–60 Three costumes by Poiret showing Oriental influence. Left, 'Robe Sorbet', 1911; centre and right, dresses of 1913

In 1913 came another startling change. Dresses no longer had collars coming up to the ears; instead there was what was known as the 'V-neck'. This created an extraordinary amount of excitement. It was denounced from the pulpit as something very like indecent exposure and by doctors as a danger to health. A blouse with a very modest triangular opening in the front was dubbed a 'pneumonia blouse', but in spite of all these protests the V-neck was soon generally accepted. The collar, if there was one, now took the form of a small medici collar at the back of the neck.

227

257 At home, 1913. The graceful mode of the period just before World War I

Pre-war fashions:

261 Day dress, 1912

262 Evening dress by
Paquin, 1913

263 Day dress, 1914

264, 265 Utility clothes, World War I

Just before the outbreak of war there was another modification in the general outline of women's dress. Over the skirt, which was very long and tight at the ankle, was worn another skirt, a kind of tunic reaching to just below the knee. The shape of hats also was modified. They were no longer excessively broad, but were small and fitted the head quite closely. Feathers, which were still fashionable, were no longer curled round the brim but stuck straight up into the air, and it was customary to wear two feathers projecting at an angle. These hats continued into the war period, but many women found the double skirt an encumbrance in the war work in which many of them were engaged. They therefore abandoned the underskirt and wore the tunic or overskirt by itself. The *Ill. 265* simple tailor-made was also popular, many women feeling, quite rightly, that extravagant dressing was out of place in wartime. The war, in fact, as all wars do, had a deadening effect

229

on fashion, and there is little of interest to record until the conflict was over. For those who lived through the clothing restrictions and coupons of World War II, it is interesting to note that, in 1918, there was an attempt to introduce a National Standard Dress, a utility garment, with metal buckles instead of hooks and eyes, and designed, to quote a contemporary, as an 'outdoor gown, house gown, rest gown, tea gown, dinner gown, evening dress and nightgown'. Nightgown is surely the only surprising item in this list.

In 1919, when fashion picked up again, the flared skirt which had lasted throughout the war was replaced by the so-called 'barrel' line. The effect was completely tubular. Skirts were still long, but an attempt was made to confine the body in a cylinder. The bust was entirely boyish, and women even began to wear 'flatteners' in order to conform to the prevailing mode. The waist disappeared altogether, and there were already many examples of the waistline round the hips which was to be so characteristic a feature of the middle of the decade.

267 Right, evening dresses, 1919

266 Day dresses, June 1919

268 Left, day dresses and velvet dress, 1921

269 Above, foulard silk summer dress, 1920

The early 1920s: the line is tubular but the skirt is still long

231

And then, in 1925, to the scandal of many, came the real revolution of short skirts. They were denounced from the pulpit in Europe and America, and the Archbishop of Naples even went so far as to announce that the recent earthquake at Amalfi was due to the anger of God against a skirt which reached no further than the knee. The secular establishment was equally disturbed, especially in America, and, undeterred by the fact that sumptuary laws have had only minimal success throughout history, the legislators of various American States tried once more to impose their own view of morality. In Utah a Bill was brought in, providing fine and imprisonment for those who wore on the streets 'skirts higher than three inches above the ankle'; and a Bill introduced into the Ohio legislature sought to prohibit any 'female over fourteen years of age' from wearing 'a skirt which does not reach that part of the foot known as the instep'. It was all to no avail.

270 Summer dresses, 1926. The short skirt and the androgyne silhouette is now established

271 Ladies at
the Ritz,
April 1926

A new type of woman had come into existence. The new
erotic ideal was androgyne: girls strove to look as much like
boys as possible. All curves – that female attribute so long
admired – were completely abandoned. And, as if to give the
crowning touch to their attempted boyishness, all young
women cut off their hair. The bob of the early 1920s was abandoned for the shingle, which made the coiffure follow much
more closely the lines of the head. Even older women were
compelled to conform, because the cloche hat, which had now
become universal, made it almost impossible to have long hair.
Early in 1927 even this was not considered enough, and the
shingle was succeeded by the Eton crop. There was now
nothing to distinguish a young woman from a schoolboy
except perhaps her rouged lips and pencilled eyebrows.

233

A curious result of the new modes was that they notably diminished, or at least threatened, the dominance of the great Paris fashion houses. The Frenchwoman does not naturally look like a boy; she did not fit into the new fashions as easily as her contemporaries in England and the United States. As a commentator of the time remarked, 'the angular English woman, over whose lack of *embonpoint* papers like *La Vie Parisienne* have been making merry for two generations, now became the accepted type of beauty'. Several famous Paris firms, such as Doucet, Doeuillet and Drécoll, who had created the glories of *la belle époque*, closed their doors; and even Poiret, who had done so much to revolutionize fashion in 1910, now found himself completely out of tune with the times. New names emerged, many of them women. Madame Paquin, although she was head of a long-established firm, managed to conform to the new trend. Madeleine Vionnet accepted it with

enthusiasm; but the outstanding revolutionary talent of the Twenties was undoubtedly 'Coco' Chanel, only rivalled a few years later by the astonishing figure of Elsa Schiaparelli. These two women were not merely dress designers; they formed an important part of the whole artistic movement of the time. Madame Chanel was an intimate friend of Cocteau, Picasso and Stravinsky. Madame Schiaparelli was fantastically success-ful, and it has been estimated that by 1930 the turnover of her establishment in the rue Cambon was something like a hundred and twenty million francs a year. Her twenty-six workrooms employed more than two thousand people.

What the fashion people found so shocking about her was her introduction of 'good working-class clothes' into polite society. She was accused of having brought the *apache* into the Ritz; but however simple her clothes might be, they always had an elegance which made everyone admire and copy them.

Ill. 274

272 Left, lady's tweed suit, 1929

273 The 'flattener', intended to abolish the bust, 1924

274 Dresses by Chanel, April 1926

275 At Chester races, 1926. Masculine elements in female costume

277 At the races, Longchamps, 1930.
The skirts are on the eve of going long
again and the waist is about to resume its
normal place

276 Afternoon coat, 1928

The function of fashion is to change, and by the end of the 1920s it was plain that a new style was about to be evolved. Skirts reached the extreme of shortness (the extreme, that is, until modern times) in 1927. It was not in everybody's interest that skirts should be short. It is true that the manufacturers of silk stockings were enjoying a boom, but the skimpy dresses of the period did not bring much profit to cloth manufacturers or the designers of accessories. It was plain that attempts were being made to bring skirts down again and, as so often happens, the first experiments were made with evening dress. Skirts remained short, but they were sometimes provided with a gauze overskirt which was somewhat longer; or long panels were added at the side. Another expedient, and an extremely ugly one, was to make the skirt longer at the back than the front. There were even examples which came down to the knees at the front and trailed on the ground behind, and this ugly and preposterous fashion lasted for nearly a year.

278 'Pierrette' hair-style by Lanvin, 1928

279 Evening dress, May 1929. At the end of the 1920s the couturiers made
definite efforts to bring in long skirts again by various devices such as
transparent hems, side-pieces and trains

Then, as the decade drew to its close, skirts suddenly became long again and the waist resumed its normal place. It was as if fashion were trying to say: 'The party is over; the Bright Young Things are dead.' As in 1820, the return of the waist to its normal position symbolized a movement towards a new paternalism: in economic terms the American Slump; in political terms the rise of Hitler. The cloche hat, which had tyrannized over the mode for nearly ten years, was abolished and women were free to grow their hair again. The long sleeves were seen once more; but there is no exact parallel between the fashions of the early 1930s and those of a century before, for the waist did not become excessively tight and the general lines of the skirt remained more or less perpendicular. Wide

280, 281 Day and evening dress by Lanvin, 1931

shoulders and slender hips seemed to be every woman's ideal, exemplified in the figure of Greta Garbo. In the 1930s, especially, film actresses were almost arbiters of fashion, their costumes created by designers such as Gilbert Adrian.

If the psychologists' theory of the Shifting Erogenous Zone can be accepted, once a focus of interest loses its appeal another one has to be found. In the early 1930s the emphasis shifted from the legs to the back. Backs were bared to the waist and, indeed, many of the dresses of the period look as if they had been designed to be seen from the rear. Even day dresses had a slit up the back, and the skirt was drawn tightly over the hips so as to reveal, perhaps for the first time in history, the shape of the buttocks.

282 Evening dress by Worth, 1930. An example of the new focus of erotic interest: a dress designed to be seen from the back

It seems likely that this backlessness had something to do with the evolution of bathing costumes. The bathing costumes of the 1920s were surprisingly modest; fashion photographs of the period show mannequins in quite ample overskirts and extremely limited décolletage. In the early 1930s all this was changed. What really brought this about, however, was not bathing, but *sunbathing*, which was now enjoying a tremendous vogue. If, as some fanatics claimed, the exposure of the skin to sunlight was the way to health for everybody, then obviously the greater portion of skin exposed the better. The overskirt of the bathing costume was therefore reduced to almost nothing, the armholes were enlarged and the décolletage was much deeper. Finally, the first backless bathing costume appeared, although, in fact, it was no more backless than the evening dress of the same period.

In addition to bathing, other sports were beginning to have a marked influence on ordinary costume, although we should note also the opposite tendency of sports clothes to develop a type of their own; this is particularly noticeable in the case of tennis. Most tennis players had simply worn the summer clothes of the period, even if the skirts were long and hampering to the movements. In the 1920s, when the skirts of ordinary dress were short, tennis costume followed suit, but when skirts became long again at the end of the decade, tennis dress went on, so to speak, on its own, since it was plainly absurd to reintroduce long skirts in what had now become a strenuous game. In April 1931 Señorita de Alvarez played in divided skirts which came to slightly below the knee, and two years later Alice Marble of San Francisco appeared in shorts above the knee. It was left to Mrs Fearnley-Whittingstall to appear at Wimbledon without stockings. This caused an uproar, but the new mode was so obviously sensible that it was soon adopted by almost all women players.

A similar evolution can be seen in skating costume, which by the early 1930s had crystallized into a kind of uniform, having a skirt with wide flares, at first knee-length but afterwards

283 Evening outfit by Edward Molyneux, 1933. The square shoulders and sleek lines of the decade are already visible.

much shorter. Cycling, although it had long ceased to have any appeal to the upper classes, was still extremely popular, and most young women adopted shorts, sometimes so short that considerable opposition was aroused when English cycling clubs went abroad.

The main lines of women's clothes in the early 1930s may be briefly summarized. Dresses were slim and straight, being sometimes wider at the shoulders than at the hips. Tall girls were admired, and all the tricks of the couturier were employed to give the impression of increased height. This effect can be *Ill. 283* increased by making the head look small, and so the hair was dressed rather close, with a small curl at the back of the neck.

284 At the races, 1930

285 Suit, 1935. An
extreme example of
the exaggerated
shoulder

286, 287 The bosom has not yet reasserted itself after the flat styles of the 1920s. Left, at the races, May 1935. Right, summer dress, 1934

On top was a gay little hat perched over one eye. Day dresses usually came to about ten inches above the ground, while evening dresses reached to the toes. Both evening and afternoon dresses were often provided with little capes. The bolero was extremely fashionable. Perhaps as a gesture of economy, evening dresses were sometimes made of woollen or cotton materials and even of broadcloth, previously thought suitable only for day wear.

Ill. 285

The Depression certainly helped to bring the clothes of the different classes closer together, at least in general line, and now a new process had begun which brought the creations of the great Paris houses within the reach of nearly every woman.

288, 289 'Butterfly' sleeve dresses, 1934

Before 1930 it had been the habit of buyers (especially American buyers) to purchase several dozen copies of each selected model shown in Paris and resell them to a wealthy clientele. But after the Slump the American authorities imposed a duty of up to 90 per cent on the cost of the original model. *Toiles* (i.e. patterns cut out in linen) were allowed in duty-free. Each *toile* was supplied with full directions for making it up, and although the original dress may have cost a hundred thousand francs, it was now possible to sell a simplified version for as little as fifty dollars. Another factor which contributed to the same end was the growing use of synthetic fabrics. Even the factory girl could now afford to purchase artificial silk stockings.

As the clouds of World War II began to gather, it became obvious that the fashionable silhouette was beginning to be modified, even if the fashion designers were as puzzled as the

246

290 Fashion shows in a salon, 1935

general public about what the dominating trend would be. There was a new wave of romanticism stimulated by the visit of the King and Queen to Paris in the early summer of 1938. 'Never', says C. Willett Cunnington, 'has Fashion been more ironic than in this attempt to revive, for an evening dress, the modes current on the eve of the Franco-Prussian War' (*English Women's Clothing in the Present Century*). There was even an attempt to revive the crinoline. Day dresses, however, showed an opposite tendency. The skirt was shorter and was bunched up in the peasant style. Curiously enough it was an *Austrian* peasant style, as if in unconscious acknowledgment of the growing power of Hitler. But right up to the eve of the conflict the majority of fashion designers, consciously or unconsciously, were betting that there would be no war. There was even an attempt to bring in tight-lacing again.

In the summer of 1939 *Vogue*'s reporter noted the extraordinary variety of models offered by the leading houses, and added: 'Nothing varies more than silhouette. You can look as different from your neighbour as the moon from the sun - and both of you are right. The only thing that you must have in common is a tiny waist, held in if necessary by super-light-weight boned and laced corsets. There isn't a silhouette in Paris that doesn't cave in at the waist.'

The accentuated waist was a boon to advertisers, who called upon women to 'control it with corsets . . . where there's a will there's a way!' Women were promised 'an old-fashioned boned, laced corset, made, by modern magic, light and persuasive as a whisper'. Perhaps, if peace had been preserved, women in the 1940s would once more have confined their waists in a rigid cage. History, however, decreed otherwise.

But for the moment it seemed that nothing had changed. Most of the great Paris houses launched their usual collections in the spring of 1940. It was the period of the 'phoney war', and no one in England or France or even America seemed to realize that the second great conflict of the twentieth century was really upon them.

292 Paris fashions, June 1939

291 At the races, 1938. Hats
during the 1930s were a little
mad in reaction against the
universal cloche of the previous
decade

293 Male fashions for
spring and summer, 1920

Men's clothes continued the progress towards informality which had been noticeable since the end of World War I. After the Armistice the frock coat had become something of a rarity, and its rival the morning coat was to be seen only at weddings, funerals or some occasion when Royalty was present. The lounge suit had now become ordinary town wear, but after 1922 it was shorter and had no slit up the back. The decay of the waistcoat led to a new increase in the popularity of double-breasted coats. The single-breasted coat, however, still continued, and in the later Twenties there was a craze for double-breasted waistcoats to go with it.

The chief change in the mid 1920s was in the width of trousers, the so-called 'Oxford bags'. It is thought that these may have originated from the extremely ample trousers made of towelling worn by undergraduate oarsmen *over* their shorts. It was customary for the coach to ride a horse along the tow-path wearing these trousers, and since he was a person of considerable prestige, undergraduates in general adopted the mode. Certainly they were to be seen everywhere, and were sometimes so wide that only the tip of the shoe was visible and the trousers flapped about the leg in the most extraordinary fashion. So strange a mode was not likely to last long, and by the end of the 1920s extremely wide 'Oxford bags' had disappeared, but trousers remained fairly wide until the end of the 1930s.

Meanwhile knickerbockers had been enjoying a renewed boom. For some obscure reason the breeches worn by Guards officers during World War I differed from the riding breeches of officers in Line Regiments by being extremely baggy and so loose as to hang over the top of the puttees. These had a strange effect on ordinary knickerbockers, which began to be cut, immediately after the war, in the same fashion, only even more amply. The new baggy knickerbockers were known as 'plus-fours', being considered especially suitable for golf. They completely drove out the old knickerbocker costume, which henceforward was worn only by old-fashioned intellectuals. They were in many ways the most typical sartorial invention of the period between the wars.

294 Examples of the new informality: left, M. Herriot in the French style; right, Mr Ramsay Macdonald in the English style, 1924

CHAPTER TEN

Rationed fashion to pluralistic style

THE Second World War had a profound impact on the fashion industries of Europe and America and consequently on the design of clothing. With the German invasion of Paris in June 1940, the international capital of fashion became cut off from the rest of the world. Chanel had already shut down the year before, and other couture houses now began to close their doors. Jacques Heim, who was Jewish, went into hiding, and Molyneux and Worth moved to England. Mainbocher and Schiaparelli left for the United States, though Schiaparelli kept her Paris salon open. Among the more than ninety houses that carried on business as usual were Lelong, Patou, Rochas, Lanvin, Ricci, Fath and Balenciaga.

Some of these couturiers showed small collections throughout the Occupation, and the design of Parisian haute couture clothing continued to evolve from the styles of the 1930s. Because rationing would be of benefit only to the occupiers, no attempt was made to conserve materials or labour and dresses were long and full-skirted. Many were corsetted and some included late-nineteenth-century revival-style bustles. They were accompanied by outlandishly tall and lavishly decorated hats.

Since none of this was visible to the outside world, Paris's hegemony of fashion effectively came to an end and the rest of Europe and North America, which had traditionally looked to the French capital for stylistic guidance and inspiration, suddenly found themselves forced to rely entirely on domestic design talent. Moreover, their designers had to meet the challenge of shortages brought about by the war.

In Britain, a rationing system was introduced in the summer of 1941, regulating the quantity of clothing which could be

252

purchased. The following year, the British Board of Trade introduced the Utility Clothing Scheme, a system of controls on the amount of fabric and number of trimmings used in clothing. The Incorporated Society of London Fashion Designers (known as Inc. Soc.) – led by Molyneux, and including among others Hardy Amies, Norman Hartnell, Digby Morton and Victor Stiebel – took on the task of creating a prototype range of clothing which met these requirements, using minimal material and labour resources. Four basic lines were produced – coat, suit, dress and blouse – from which thirty-two individual designs were selected for manufacture. These were mass produced and bore the CC41 Utility label. The look was simple but stylish, with good proportion and line. It *Ill.295* incorporated padded shoulders, a nipped-in waist and hems to just below the knee.

295 Typical U.K. wartime outfit: tailored suit with square shoulders, nipped-in waist and skirt reaching just below the knee, teamed with a small hat and functional bag and shoes. It was a style that gave civilian women a somewhat military appearance

Textiles were also strictly controlled. Because silk was needed to make parachutes, there was a ban on its use for hosiery and clothing. Nylon, introduced by Du Pont in America in 1939, was not yet widely available, so manufacturers offered stockings in rayon, cotton and wool. When these materials also became difficult to obtain, women took to wearing ankle socks in the summer months or, when all else failed, staining their legs and drawing a mock seam down the back of the calf. The stockings shortage helped to increase the popularity of trousers, which were enthusiastically adopted by many younger women working in factories and on the land.

In an attempt to counteract the severity of the Utility lines, dress fabrics were brightly coloured, though printed and woven repeat patterns were kept small to avoid wastage when cutting. *Ill. 296* A government campaign known as 'Make-do and Mend' encouraged women accustomed to discarding worn or out-moded clothing to re-make and update it. Despite the fact that hats were unrationed, many women preferred to wear turbans, snoods and headscarves.

In 1940 in the United States, the isolation from Paris coincided with an exploitation of domestic talent. Mainbocher – the first American designer to run a successful house in the French capital – was back in New York, as was Charles James. Two new talents also appeared on the scene: Norman Norell and Claire McCardell, both of whom had worked with Hattie Carnegie, the country's best-known ready-to-wear designer. Throughout the war years, Norell showed many simple yet sophisticated designs, including in 1942 his trendsetting sequinned evening sheaths (using unrationed sequins). The field of sportswear, in which the United States was to excel, found its quintessential exponent in McCardell, whose hallmarks were simplicity and practicality. When in 1942 the American War Production Board (WPB) imposed limits (the L85 laws) on the use of certain textiles required for the war effort – mainly wool and silk – McCardell turned to cotton, using denim, seersucker, ticking and jersey to produce a range of attractive, easy-to-wear

254

Go through your wardrobe

296 A British Second World War propaganda poster urges women to economize and be resourceful in order to conserve scarce clothing resources

designs, many of which have become classics. Her wrap-around 'popover' dress, first shown in 1942, continued to be produced throughout her career.

Although restrictions in America affected many aspects of dress – the cut of men's suits, width of women's skirts, heights of heels, colour of shoe leather, etc. – they were not as stringent as those in effect in Britain. Moreover, they did not last so long: restrictions came to an end in the United States in 1946 but rationing dragged on in Britain until 1948.

By the end of the war, British and American designers had a much sharper international profile. In both countries, too, significant developments had been made in the area of ready-to-wear clothing. Mass-market manufacturers had improved their skills – often in the mass production of uniforms. In America, the WPB sponsored a nationwide survey of women's measurements from which to create basic guidelines for much-needed standardized sizing.

In the immediate postwar years, both Britain and the United States hoped to lead world fashion, but neither was to succeed. After the Liberation, Paris couturiers abandoned the brazen extravagance of the years of Occupation and returned to a simpler look. But the French couture establishment knew that it needed to win back overseas buyers, especially those from the United States, who now felt less tied to Paris and its influence. In 1945, in a push to revive the couture industry, French artists and designers collaborated to produce the Théâtre de la Mode, an exhibition of wire-frame miniature mannequins dressed in couture clothing – precise copies of the Spring/Summer collections of that year – which was used to publicize French fashion as it travelled to London, Barcelona, Stockholm, Copenhagen and several cities in America.

During the postwar years, Balmain, Balenciaga and Dior were to emerge as the most eminent of Parisian designers. The latter was to put the French capital firmly back at the centre of the fashion map in February 1947, when, as a newly independent designer, he showed his first collection, the Corolle line. Immediately nicknamed the New Look, it was to achieve unprecedented attention worldwide, not all of it favourable.

The New Look was in fact not new at all, but simply an exaggeration of late 1930s and Occupation styles, yet it was the very antithesis of the clothing produced in both the UK and the <ill>Ill. 297</ill> United States during the war. Soft, rounded shoulders emphasized the breasts; waists were heavily corsetted; hips were padded. Skirts – and herein lay the scandal – were billowing, reaching almost to the ankle. Most used as many as fifteen yards of fabric.

To much of the war-weary population, the New Look symbolized hopes for a more prosperous future. Others saw it as reckless waste at a time when fabric was still in short supply. Some women feared that its anachronistic, prewar shape – its out-and-out femininity – heralded a return by women to a less active role in society. But, despite the mixed response, it was eventually to win general support and would dominate the design of women's clothing until 1954.

Throughout the 1950s, women wanted to appear mature, elegant and sophisticated. High fashion remained formal, with etiquette demanding special clothes and accessories for every

297 Archetypal New Look elegance: Patricia 'Bambi' Tuckwell in a
corsetted, full-skirted cocktail dress by Christian Dior, 1949

occasion. Tailored suits, twinsets and shirtwaister dresses were worn during the day and cocktail dresses and immaculately constructed full-length gowns for evening. Perfect grooming was essential at all times. Most women either wore their hair in a softly waved pageboy or had regular perms, to achieve one of the shorter, curly styles. Chignons and french pleats were also popular. Make-up was heavy: a pale base was highlighted with rouged cheekbones; eyebrows were finely arched; eyes were accentuated with dark liner, coloured eye-shadow and mascara; lips were stained dark red.

Though the basic fashion silhouette remained the same throughout the early years of the decade, this was a period of intense fashion activity, with top designers creating new collections twice a year. As the decade progressed, clothing became less structured and straighter in cut – a development that can be seen subtly taking place in Dior's collections of mid-decade, which included the H-line, the A-line and the Y-line. In *Ill. 299* 1954 Chanel reopened her house and reintroduced her relaxed, wearable suits and dresses, with hemlines reaching just below the knee. Balenciaga also rebelled against the lines of the New Look, showing tunic tops over long, straight skirts and softly tailored suits with stand-away collars and three-quarter-length sleeves. In 1957 he introduced the 'chemise' or sack dress, a shape which was to be taken up by other designers, including *Ill. 298* Givenchy and Jacques Griffe, and which would become the dominant line of the 1960s.

In America, most custom designers, including Norell, James Galanos, Pauline Trigère, Valentina and Anne Klein, were branching out into ready-to-wear. Claire McCardell continued to produce her stylish denim and cotton seersucker wrap-over dresses and dirndl skirts, and introduced jersey pedal-pushers with matching tops so short that they bared the midriff.

In the field of elegant sun- and swimwear, America excelled, especially in one-piece swimwear. Two-piece swimsuits were less widely worn, and though the bikini was introduced in France as early as 1946 and became popular there in the

298, 299 By the later 1950s designers were reacting against the tight-waisted, full-skirted style of the post-war years and had begun to present less structured clothing. The 'sack' dress, shown left in the 1958 version by Jacques Griffe, was to take over as the prevailing look of the next decade. Chanel's easy-fitting suit, reintroduced in 1954, also provided more comfort and wearability. The style was to prove a classic. The example above is from 1960

following decade, it was not commonly seen in the United States until the mid-sixties. American women often looked to Hollywood's film stars for inspiration, with Doris Day offering a 'girl-next-door' look and Elizabeth Taylor a more overtly sexual image.

The 1950s also witnessed the rise of Italian designers. Emilio Pucci was noted for his bold prints in swirling abstract patterns and acidic colours from which he created elegant tapered trouser suits and shift dresses. Roberto Capucci made his name as a master of form, producing dramatic, sculptural dresses and ballgowns. Italy also led the world in fashion footwear and other fine leathers.

In the field of postwar menswear, the most dramatic development took place in Britain, where, in 1953, young working-class men began to adopt the 'Edwardian' style of dress that had been introduced by Savile Row tailors in the late 1940s. The 'teddy boys' took this upper-class, somewhat dandified look - the chief elements of which were a long draped jacket and narrow 'drainpipe' trousers – and exaggerated it, adding crepe-soled shoes and narrow 'maverick' ties. What was important in this development was not the adoption by the working class of an upper-class style, but the fact that young men from poor backgrounds could now afford relatively expensive clothes and accessories and had the confidence to make them part of their own distinctive style.

In the 1950s a separate market came into being catering specifically to young people with large disposable incomes. Although many teenagers wore the same style of dress as their parents, there was in general a pronounced relaxation of dress codes among the young. Hollywood film stars James Dean and Marlon Brando popularized jeans and the motorbike jacket and also transformed the T-shirt into a fashionable item of clothing. There was a vogue for sideburns and greased hairstyles.

Teenage girls wore tight sweaters and cardigans over pointed brassières, with circular skirts held out stiffly by layers of nylon petticoats. Tight trousers or jeans with oversize jumpers were also popular with both sexes as part of the art school/beatnik look, which featured large quantities of black. Young people around the globe danced to the new American rock 'n' roll music, and it was from this date that the fashion and music industries became inextricably linked.

From the mid-1950s, Italian clothing – tailored menswear in particular - began to represent the ultimate in modernity. Soon, Italian clothes were imported into Britain and America, and domestic tailors proudly proclaimed that their own versions of these short-cut, single-breasted suits with tapered trousers were in the 'Italian style'. These were worn with narrow – often horizontally striped – ties and fine quality, Italian leather shoes, with pointed toes.

The 1960s can be split into two distinct periods. The first embraces the years 1960 to 1967 ('the swinging sixties'), when fashion focused almost entirely on youth. Though Paris continued to lead in couture and at the most exclusive levels of ready-to-wear, London spearheaded the design and retailing of fashionable teenage styles. The boutique became the dominant retail fashion outlet, providing an enticing combination of small runs of up-to-the minute clothes, young, fashionably dressed assistants, loud pop music and gimmicky interiors.

The chief fashion story of the period was the miniskirt. *Ill. 300* Hemlines rose just above the knee in 1961 and had reached the upper thighs by 1966. Stockings and suspenders were replaced by brightly coloured tights, and underwear was reduced to brief, unstructured bras and pants.

It was a style best suited to a skinny, pre-pubescent physique – epitomized by the schoolgirl model Lesley Hornby, known as Twiggy. And despite the much publicized sexual revolution, young women of this period often looked like children, in baby-doll dresses with puffed sleeves, schoolgirl pinafores and gymslips, knickerbockers and the ubiquitous miniskirt.

The designer most often credited with introducing the 'mini' was Mary Quant, who had opened her boutique 'Bazaar' in *Ill. 301* London's King's Road in 1955. Rejecting the constraints of

261

seasonal shows, she produced as many as twenty-eight collections during her early years, creating simple, practical, often mix 'n' match designs which had an element of classlessness perfectly suited to the mood of the sixties. Other designers of the new generation who made their names creating stylish fashions for the affluent youth market included Ossie Clark, Bill Gibb, Marian Foale, Sally Tuffin and Jean Muir.

It was a period when designers of both clothes and textiles celebrated modernity and scientific progress. Space-age silvers and whites were mixed with primary colours. Pop and Op Art had a profound influence on textile design. New fashion materials were introduced, including shiny, wet-look PVC, easy-care acrylics and polyesters.

Women wore their hair either long and straight or cut short (ideally by Vidal Sassoon) into a sculpted bob or wedge. Foundation and lipstick were pale, eyes enlarged with eyeliner and dark eyeshadow.

Men's clothing also received attention from inventive young designers during the 1960s, becoming more informal, more flamboyant, and notably more colourful. 'Hipster' trousers, high-collared shirts and 'kipper' ties were fashionable. Jeans remained popular and denim was also used for shirts, jackets and hats. Teenagers and students patronized army-and-navy surplus clothing outlets. Vince, opened by Bill Green in 1954, was one of the first menswear boutiques in West Soho. The shop's continental-style clothes were specifically aimed at gay men and were also available through their mail-order catalogue. Three years later the influential menswear designer John Stephen opened the first of his chain of cutting-edge menswear boutiques in Carnaby Street. He was initially patronized by Mods – the dominant subcultural group of the time – who favoured the modern 'Italian style'. By 1962 West Soho had become famous for its small specialist menswear shops, *Ill. 308* including John Paul's 'I Was Lord Kitchener's Valet', which sold ex-military uniforms and clothing emblazoned with Union Jack designs.

300 Sixties top model Jean
Shrimpton in a lace mini-dress
with matching lace tights,
1965

301 Mary Quant's simple
checked mini-dress with
dropped waist, mid-1960s

Although American men were generally more conservative – the most common outfit being a combination of Ivy-League-style tapered trousers and three-button single-breasted jacket – some concessions to the new trends were apparent by the mid-sixties.

The most extreme 1960s fashions were shown by Paris designers André Courrèges, Paco Rabanne, Pierre Cardin, Emanuel Ungaro and Yves Saint Laurent. Courrèges' Spring/ Summer 1964 'Space Age' collection featured 'astronaut' hats and goggles, white and silver PVC 'moon girl' loon trousers, *Ill. 303* catsuits and white patent or kid leather, mid-calf-length boots. Courrèges' clothes and those of Ungaro and Cardin were precision cut and unadorned. Paco Rabanne was noted for his unconventional use of materials: his first 'body jewelry' collection in 1966 consisted of shift dresses constructed from plastic or metal discs and tiles, linked with wire or chain. Yves Saint Laurent, who had designed at Dior, started under his own

302, 303 Left, see-through dress by Rudi Gernreich, 1964. Below, futuristic black-and-white gabardine outfit by André Courrèges, also featuring the designer's trend-setting white boots, 1965

name in 1962, and became an iconoclast of 1960s style, reflecting
Left-Bank influences and contemporary art movements. Copies
of his 1965 'Mondrian' dress, composed of bold blocks of   *Ill. 307*
colour, appeared in high street shops within days.

Fashion was also becoming increasingly unisex, reflecting a
gradual breaking down of long-established traditions of gender
dressing. For the first time men and women shopped at the same
boutique for jeans, trousers, jackets, sweaters and shirts. In Paris
in 1966 Yves Saint Laurent launched his famous 'smoking'
jacket for women, followed in 1967 by his knickerbocker suit, a   *Ill. 304*
year later by culottes and in 1969 by his trouser suit.   *Ills. 305, 306*

By the mid-1960s ready-to-wear was dominant. Designers
acknowledged that many young women did not want to spend
time having lengthy couture fittings, or pay high prices for
clothing that they intended to wear for a short period only. The
traditional couture clientele continued to patronize Dior (where
Marc Bohan had taken over from Saint Laurent), Balenciaga,

304–306 Yves Saint Laurent designs from the 1960s: left to right,
knickerbocker suit, 1967; culottes, 1968; trouser suit based on the cut of
menswear, 1969

307 Art has often
influenced fashion,
though rarely as directly
as in Yves Saint
Laurent's 1965 cocktail
dress, inspired by a
painting by Mondrian

Lanvin and Chanel. The master couturier Balenciaga retired in 1968, recognizing that a market no longer existed for his fine couture.

From 1968 the optimistic social and economic climate of the early 1960s started to fade as unemployment and inflation rose, most notably in Britain. People began to question the human and environmental consequences of technology and women began to rebel against imposed ideals of feminine beauty.

Fashion has sometimes been criticized for lacking direction in the years following the 'swinging sixties', the period from the late 1960s to the mid-1970s. But it was in fact this period which paved the way for the stylistic pluralism of the present day.

308 The menswear shop 'I Was Lord Kitchener's Valet' opened in Carnaby Street, Soho, in the early 1960s. This photograph, taken outside the shop towards the end of the decade, shows the mini-skirt at its upper-thigh level. Courrèges' influence is still visible in the woman's boots. The man's trousers demonstrate the wide cut of the late 1960s and early 1970s

Individuality and self-expression were paramount. Clothing was often customized with embroidered, appliquéd and patchworked designs. Tie-dye T-shirts became popular. Colours were muted and textiles predominantly made from natural fibres. In Britain, at the top end of the market, Bill Gibb became famous for his stunning appliquéd and embroidered designs and Zandra Rhodes for her exquisite, ethereal, hand-screened silk *Ill. 309* and chiffon garments. In Italy the Missonis did much to elevate the status of knitwear in fashion, incorporating subtle patterns and blends of colour.

The ethnic look predominated. Hippies were the first to adopt Afghan coats, fringed suede garments, kaftans, headbands and beads as part of their rejection of Western consumerist society. And as European and American societies became increasingly multi-cultural, the clothes and hairstyles of Afro-Caribbean, Asian and African-American communities injected a lively new ingredient into all levels of Western dress.

In the late 1960s hemlines dropped to mid-calf, a move resisted by many women, who continued to wear the miniskirt. The full-length maxi, however, which was introduced in 1969, was widely adopted. From 1971 shorts with bibs and straps – popularly known as 'hotpants' – offered an alternative to the mini. By the following year skirts and dresses had become longer, fluid and more romantic, and the 'futuristic' fashions of the early 1960s had given way to nostalgia.

Styles of the 1930s in particular were revived, with many designers cutting their clothing on the bias and exploiting fluid fabrics, especially satins. In London's Kensington, Barbara *Ill. 310* Hulanicki's new art deco emporium, Biba, which opened in 1973, exulted in pastiche 1930s Hollywood glamour. Authentic period clothing also became desirable and specialist shops

309 This handpainted and handprinted dress from Zandra Rhodes typifies the move in the 1970s away from the rather geometric futuristic look of the previous decade towards a more loose and flowing style. Ethnic elements are also beginning to enter high fashion

310, 311 A nostalgia for 1930s styling is revealed both in Barbara
Hulanicki's early 1970s designs for Biba, above left, and in Jean Muir's
fluid dress design of 1973, above right

opened to cater to this demand. A 1940s influence was apparent
in both men's and women's shoes, which were designed with
dangerously high platform soles from the early to the
mid-1970s.

In the United States in 1971, Ralph Lauren, who had made his
name with his 'Polo' line for men, produced a line of tailored
suits for women. Calvin Klein also designed stylish women's
clothes along masculine lines.

In the early 1970s trousers were cut very wide, into 'flares' or
'bags'. 'Flares', which subsequently became the chief symbol of
the fashion of the period, were tight around the thigh and
widened from the knee downward. 'Bags' were loose, reminis-
cent of 1920s and 1930s styles. From 1975, trousers were cut
narrow and straight.

269

By the early 1970s, the first wave of Japanese designers had arrived in Paris. Challenging Western traditions of tailoring, Kenzo (Takada) and Issey Miyake presented an approach to dressing which concentrated on layering and wrapping, swathing the body in loose, unstructured garments. Kenzo introduced peasant-style, wide-legged drawstring trousers, quilted jackets and tabards. Miyake's inspired, uncompromising clothing was constructed by working his fabrics directly onto the body, to create softly sculptural garments.

Ill. 312   The anarchic Punk style, which appeared on the streets of London during the mid-1970s, and which spread in diluted form throughout Europe and North America, was to have an enormous impact on both streetwear and high fashion. It was a style which consciously sought to shock, combining – for both sexes – black tight trousers and striped mohair sweaters with

312 Punks in London's King's Road, 1980. Although Punk was a visually menacing and provocative youth style, it was to have a widespread and lasting influence on all levels of dress, including high fashion. Elements of the Punk look continued to appear on catwalks throughout the 1980s and into the 1990s

313 Vivienne Westwood, creator of much of Punk style, began to show her collections in 1981. Underwear worn as outerwear featured in her influential Buffalo collection of Autumn/Winter 1982/83

customized leather jackets and heavy-duty Doctor Marten boots. Some female Punks wore miniskirts, fishnet tights and high stiletto-heeled shoes. Fetishistic leather and rubber were an integral part of the Punk look, as were trousers with bondage straps from knee to knee, and bondage collars. Clothes were slashed and ripped, embellished with safety pins, zips and studs. T-shirts were printed with aggressive, anarchistic slogans. The most famous retail outlet for Punk garments and accessories was the shop Seditionaries in London's King's Road, run by Vivienne Westwood and Malcolm McLaren – key figures in the visual styling of the Punk movement.

   In complete contrast to the artificially pale and unhealthy look of the Punks, there was a strong swing in the late 1970s

271

314, 315 Above left, Issey Miyake's layered look from 1982, comprising wrap, shirt and dirndl skirt. Above right, sweater and skirt from Norma Kamali's innovative and influential 'Sweats' collection of Spring/Summer 1981, based on dance and exercise clothing

towards health and personal fitness. Dance studios and gyms sprang up throughout Europe and North America and specialist clothing became an integral part of this trend. In the late 1970s the American designer Norma Kamali was instrumental in bringing sportswear into the fashion arena, introducing sweat-shirting ra-ra skirts, bandeau tops, jumpsuits, leotards and leggings. Stretchy Lycra yarns, developed by Du Pont in 1959, were in use by the 1970s and did much to improve the appearance and fit of sports and fashion clothes. Another significant originator of the sportswear trend was the reggae musician Bob Marley, who appeared on stage in football gear and tracksuits from the late 1970s. By the early 1980s tracksuits

Ill. 315

and training shoes had become a fashionable uniform among young urban black youth and were subsequently adopted by both sexes and all ages, as comfortable leisure wear.

At the top end of the fashion trade, the boom years of the early 1980s witnessed a dramatic rise in the demand for luxurious haute-couture and ready-to-wear clothing. Much of this increased business came from wealthy Americans as well as from a new, oil-rich Middle-Eastern market. At this time fashion was still clearly directional, with seasonal trends publicized by an ever-expanding international fashion media. In the main, styles were either short and fitted or voluminous and layered.

For evening, many of the more traditional Parisian houses, such as Balmain, Dior and Givenchy, revived the structured, highly decorated garments for which they had always been known. Thierry Mugler and Azzedine Alaïa offered a more *Ills. 317, 316* youthful, bold and overtly sexual image, producing clinging, body-conscious clothes, which sometimes drew on fetishistic corsetry and lacing.

At the House of Chanel – that bastion of the Establishment – dramatic changes were made with the appointment of Karl Lagerfeld as designer in 1983. Lagerfeld's brief was to increase

316 Azzedine Alaïa started showing his collections in 1981. From the beginning he focused on the shape of the female form, producing body-hugging, clinging garments which were overtly sexual in their appeal. This dress, made even more revealing by the use of side-lacing, is from his Spring/Summer 1986 collection

sales by attracting a new, youthful market, while retaining the loyalty of Chanel's traditional customers. From the outset he exploited Chanel's signature designs, sometimes paying *Ill. 318* homage to her classic styles and at other times parodying them without mercy. Within a year the House of Chanel was once again in the forefront of fashion.

For daytime, padded-shouldered suits – with trousers as well as skirts – became the mainstay 'power-dressing' wardrobe for the professional woman and it was in this field that the Italians excelled. Milan had been established as Italy's fashion capital by the mid-1970s and Italian designers continued to be acknowledged for their specialist use of textiles. In 1982 Gianni Versace worked with a modernistic, pliant metallic mesh and in the same year Giorgio Armani created an international vogue for crumpled suit and dress fabrics, particularly linen. Franco Moschino gained a reputation as the bad boy of Italian fashion, *Ill. 319* with his irreverent collections featuring dresses covered with bras or teddy bears.

275 Above, Moschino's advertising campaign for Autumn/Winter
1988/89 featured Violetta Sanchez modelling the designer's
famous teddy-bear dress

317, 318 Opposite far left, Thierry Mugler's
vampish tailored suit pays homage to glamorous
femininity, Autumn/Winter 1989/90. Opposite left,
Karl Lagerfeld continues the Chanel tradition of
tweeds and leather-entwined chains, but teams them
with white cotton Y-fronts, Spring/Summer 1993

320, 321 Above left, Ralph Lauren's 1982 outfit of raw silk jacket and linen culottes looks back to the early 20th century. Above right, Calvin Klein brought masculine tailoring to womenswear in these broad-shouldered tuxedo coats for Autumn/Winter 1983/84

In America there was a move towards a traditional look for *Ill. 320* both men and women. Ralph Lauren, Perry Ellis and later *Ill. 321* Calvin Klein created fashions which often embodied the style of 1920s British aristocrats and American pioneers, a highly successful formula which they have retained to the present day. Donna Karan dressed the businesswoman in comfortable, stylish and versatile clothes for all times of day.

The 1980s also saw many designers expand their ranges to embrace menswear. These included Mugler (1980), Comme des Garçons (1983), Jean-Paul Gaultier (1984) and Karl Lagerfeld (1989). With this trend came special menswear shows and designer collectives, such as the Fifth Circle Group in London, whose members included Joe Casely-Hayford and John Richmond. Running parallel with seasonal changes in menswear, and

276

headline-hitting styles such as Gaultier's sarongs for men, was the continued popularity of 'authentic' American workwear, collegiate Preppy styles and sportswear at all market levels.

The clothes of innovative Japanese designers, who continued to show in Paris, offered a stark and often startling alternative to Western styles. The second wave of Japanese designers, including Yohji Yamamoto and Rei Kawakubo of Comme des *Ill. 322* Garçons, began to show their collections in Paris in the late 1970s and early 1980s. Their oversize garments for men and women were often cut asymmetrically, with oddly positioned sleeves and pockets. Predominant colours were black, ink blue, neutral creams and beige with a hint of bright red. Some garments were inspired by traditional Japanese ceremonial clothes and workwear, while others celebrated modernity. Designs ranged from T-shaped garments in indigo-blue linens to Issey Miyake's moulded silicone bustiers in bright primary colours. However, on the whole, Japanese designer clothes

322 The unstructured Japanese look continued in this oversize design from Rei Kawakubo of Comme des Garçons, Autumn/ Winter 1983/84. Kawakubo favoured black and dark blue and used mainly natural materials

were, and still are, characterized by their loose fit, which conceals the natural contours of the body.

Paris has held on to its international fashion status and, in addition to Japanese designers, many European couturiers also present their collections there. These include Britain's Vivienne Westwood and Hussein Chalayan, the Belgian designers Dries van Noten and Raf Simons and the experimental Dutch duo Viktor & Rolf. France has always supported and actively promoted her fashion industry and the opportunities for high-profile licensing agreements which fund the fashion houses are still ripest in Paris. Fashion houses, often headed by international conglomerates, make substantial financial losses on their haute couture collections, but these highly publicized, glamour-laden events provide the label prestige which makes their

323–327 From opposite left, clockwise, Giorgio Armani's broad-shouldered tailored suit for Spring/Summer 1989; Missoni knitwear in signature shades for Autumn/Winter 1987/88; stark simplicity from Yohji Yamamoto, Spring/Summer 1989; teddy-boy-style suits in bold checks from Paul Smith, Spring/Summer 1994; Christian Lacroix's drawing for his 'Bazar' collection, Autumn/Winter 1994/95

328 Left, Christian Lacroix's fascination with historical dress is revealed in this short, puff skirt – an abbreviated crinoline – shown in his first independent collection in the Summer of 1987

329, 330 Opposite left, 'tribal style' model and clothes, including a sarong, at Jean-Paul Gaultier's Paris catwalk show, Spring/Summer 1994. Opposite right, Anna Sui exploits ethnicity, futuristic cyber looks and 1970s styling for her Spring/Summer 1994 collection

numerous licensed goods so commercially lucrative. Diffusion lines, consumer products, and – most significantly of all – perfume sales, continue to earn top designers high salaries.

From 1986 the fashion industries suffered another slump, but as always there remained a small, wealthy and discerning clientele for exquisitely made, beautiful clothing. Christian Lacroix, who opened his Paris house in 1986, recognized this market sector and catered to it. From the outset he championed the revival of the traditional crafts so central to the art of haute *Ill. 328* couture. His sumptuous clothes for day and evening often reflected his passion for historical dress translated into a modern idiom. The beading and embroidery workshops, the makers of buttons, *passementerie* and craft textiles enjoyed a significant rise in business through his much publicized shows.

Sales for international couture and ready-to-wear gradually started to pick up in the early 1990s. At the same time came the rise of a new generation of young, avant-garde designers, including the Belgians Martin Margiela and Ann Demeulemeester, the Austrian Helmut Lang, the Swedish designer Marcel Marongui, the African Xuly-Bet and the French designer Martine Sitbon. Drawing on 1970s styling and early 1980s Japanese designer collections, they spearheaded a new movement, popularly known as deconstructivism. Deconstructivist garments were generally black and were designed either oversize or shrunken, or so as to appear to be inside-out, with uneven hemlines and (beautifully finished) exposed seams and slashes. Since the overall look was distressed, parallels with the economic recession were inevitable, as were suggestions that new designers were paving the way for the new century.

In the course of the 1990s, dramatic changes took place. A greater range of styles than ever before came on offer. Magazines no longer presented the forthcoming season's trend: instead, they revealed the variety of themes, shapes and textiles that had emerged. The first half of the decade saw the reintroduction of 1960s and 1970s revival styles (from miniskirts and flares to Hippy styles, platforms and Punk), futuristic cyberpunk looks, *Ill. 330* eco fashions, ethnic styles, grunge, school uniforms and sports- *Ill. 329*

wear and an array of upgraded subcultural style, such as catwalk Teddy Boys, Surfers, Ragga and B-Boys. The preponderance of retro encouraged the spread of second-hand clothing shops, selling American workwear and period styles for the fashion-conscious, and cheap, durable clothing for the less well-off.

As the decade progressed, an increasingly confused fashion industry became ever more reliant on pastiche and literal updates of significant looks from earlier decades. Designers were now often perceived as stylists, able to reinterpret classic ideas for a more and more diverse market, one controlled as much by marketing and advertising budgets as by creativity.

The most successful and influential fashion development of the period was the rise of Gucci, established in Milan in 1906 as a saddlery house. This brand showed how a traditional luxury goods house could reinvent itself through the introduction of a new designer and a high-octane publicity campaign. The company's fortunes began their upward turn in 1988, when the

331, 332 The Milanese house Gucci exerted considerable influence on mass market fashion in the late 1990s with designs such as its feather-trim jeans and floral print ruffle dress, both from the Spring/Summer 1999 collection

founder's grandchildren sold their interest to an investment company, which in turn began a succession of new appointments, culminating in 1994 in that of US designer Tom Ford, under whose direction Gucci became by the mid-nineties the world's most desirable luxury label. Ford recognized that high-profile advertising combined with dynamic show presentations could boost the sales of the company's more lucrative goods such as the famous snaffle loafers and logo belts and bags. But it was Gucci's clothing range which – though an adjunct to the accessories – had the broadest influence on international fashion: the iconic pieces from this period, such as the collarless biker jacket of Spring/Summer 1998, and the feather-embroidered jeans and oversized floral print dresses of Spring/Summer 1999, inspired an avalanche of copies by the mass market. The rebirth of Gucci is emblematic of the growing number of luxury conglomerates investing in the fashion business.

Ills. 331–2

The late 1990s also witnessed other important new design appointments. The British designer Alexander McQueen, best known for popularizing a look known as 'Agro Chic', which entailed low-slung 'bumster' trousers and aggressively linear tailoring that exaggerated both waist and shoulder, was appointed at Givenchy, where he remained until 2001. His compatriot John Galliano, whose designs are based on pastiches of historic dress or, more specifically, historic figures who act as both muse and inspiration for intensely complex, decorative and showy creations, went to Dior. The Americans Marc Jacobs and Michael Kors joined leather houses Louis Vuitton and Celine, while the Belgian designer Martin Margiela moved to Hermès.

Ill. 334

Ill. 333

If the reinvention of the classic design house has become a leitmotif of the designer industry at the turn of the millennium, the major creative movements in fashion in the 1990s were inspired as much by the street as the catwalk, as the boundaries between the two fields became increasingly blurred. The mid-nineties saw the impact of designers such as the Austrian Helmut Lang, whose knack of appropriating non-fashion classics such as army surplus for a designer-literate clientele

Ill. 335

333, 334 John Galliano and Alexander McQueen have gained reputations through their innate sense of theatre, both in show presentations and in evening wear. Above left, John Galliano for Dior Couture, Spring/Summer 1997; above right, Alexander McQueen, Spring/Summer 2001

sanitized basic garments such as the parka and multi-pocketed cargo pant by executing them in luxury fabrics.

Lang's perception that utility clothing could be sold under a banner of luxury gave rise to a whole new industry which derived its profile from a range of garments that traditionally had little, if any, fashion connotations. Known as urban sportswear, this predominantly unisex look took army surplus and workwear ideas and combined them with some of the latest technical innovations in fabrics such as microfibre and Tencel while putting a fashion twist on silhouettes usually found in garments worn for outdoor pursuits such as snowboarding and mountaineering.

Key stylistic elements of this movement included funnelnecked parkas, oversized combat trousers and the one-strap rucksack. American retailer The Gap, founded in San Francisco in 1969, universalized the popularity of garments such as the hooded sweatshirt and cargo pant (the latter contributing to a massive downsizing in the denim market), making once-basic items a wardrobe staple for all generations.

The prevalence of urban sportswear in male dress can also be directly correlated to the increasingly informal approach to workplace clothing. Jeans and sweatshirts became acceptable during the mid-nineties in all but the most formal industries, as 'Friday wear' began to extend its influence throughout the week. Conversely, as the call for readymade suits began to dwindle, the market for high calibre made-to-measure suiting grew in response to design innovations from a new generation of bespoke tailors. In Britain Timothy Everest, Richard James and Ozwald Boateng brought a more exuberant approach *Ill. 336* to tailoring. Their success ran parallel to the continued international strength of the German firm Hugo Boss and the Italian house of Armani.

The increasing similarities between street and catwalk culture also revealed themselves in the resurgence of proactive sports-

335, 336 Below left, Helmut Lang transforms the traditional parka into a luxurious example of urban sportswear, Autumn/Winter 1998. Below right, a boldly coloured linen suit from Ozwald Boateng, Spring/Summer 2001

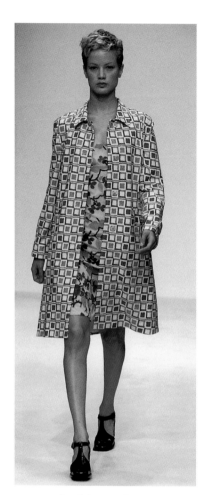

337, 338 Prada's use of print and motif inspired the mass market to emulate their designs in numerous less expensive renditions. The lime and chocolate colour palette, above left, of Spring/Summer 1996, was highly influential. Above right, the chinoiserie motif popularized Chinese satin and made versions of the traditional cheongsam stylish, Spring/Summer 1997

wear as fashion. American designer Tommy Hilfiger epitomized the heavily logoed casual-wear aesthetic of the mid- to late nineties in easily identifiable collections denoted by heavy branding.

The power of branding has influenced fashion throughout the decades, from the earliest Louis Vuitton monogrammed luggage at the beginning of the century, through the intertwined CC of Chanel and the Mary Quant daisy of the sixties, but no label did more to popularize logos in the mid-nineties than Prada, a Milanese accessory house which, like Gucci, transformed itself from a reputable leather goods manufacturer into a leading global fashion power. Headed by Miuccia Prada, granddaughter of the founder, it adopted an unusually intellectual approach to dress, gaining its initial following early in the decade for its use of nylon for handbags and raincoats at a time when fashion was enjoying a long affair with eco-friendly natural fibres. In addition to fabrication, the company's triangular metal logo, originally used to monogram luggage, became a staple of the Prada house style and spawned cheap imitations worldwide. *Ills. 337–8*

Prada's espousal of nylon is symptomatic of the new uses designers were finding for increasingly sophisticated synthetic fabrics. The manmade fibre revolution of the sixties laid the groundwork for the complex textiles available at the beginning of the twenty-first century, when, for example, new, non-creasing linens began to replace their crinkled counterparts, increasingly sophisticated fake fur encroached on the market for the real thing and designers worked more with new print technology such as ink jet printing and laser-cutting.

The relentless speed at which technology changes the landscape of daily life has had inevitable repercussions on fashion. Live web feeds have enabled designers to broadcast their catwalk presentations online as they take place, thus instantly reaching a global market far larger than the traditional fashion show audience. At the same time, the Internet has created unprecedented access to fashion information, much of which has made the process of copying designer garments so easy that the more unscrupulous among the chain stores can introduce facsimiles onto the high street before the originals are delivered to more upmarket outlets.

Stylistically, the single most important key look in womenswear to emerge since the mid-1990s was 'Modern

Ill. 339

Ill. 340

Bohemian', a style originated by the London retailer Voyage. From 1996 to the end of the decade, the bohemian look became the overriding trend within womenswear at all market levels, incorporating the adapted ethnic embroideries of Belgian designer Dries Van Noten, the bold colour sense of young British designer Matthew Williamson and the irreverent mixtures of fabrics from Milanese design houses such as Marni and Fendi. It was a trend based on mixing and layering: combining garments such as shrunken cardigans and dresses worn over trousers, clashing colours such as cerise and orange and multitudinous forms of decoration, including velvet trims, embroidered motifs, mirror appliqués and minuscule floral or paisley prints.

As fashion dallied with romanticism, a new market began to develop in tandem with Hippy chic: the fashion essential or 'must-have' item, promoted heavily through the growing number of fashion publications. Once-obscure pieces such as the pashmina shawl became highly desirable accessories. Imported from Kashmir in Northern India, the pashmina, which initially began life as a security blanket for fashion editors on long-haul flights, soon became a replacement for the scarf, materializing in numerous guises, from the costly original to cheaper blends masquerading as the real thing.

In terms of both influence and sales, the power of the accessory was the most telling indication of the direction fashion was pursuing at the beginning of the new century. Inspired by the successes of Gucci and Prada, every other house of note launched and continues to promote handbag, footwear or *Ill. 341* sunglasses collections that enable consumers to buy into the designer dream on a limited budget. Cult handbags such as the Fendi 'baguette' accumulated a readymade waiting list from *Ill. 342* eager customers keen to display what had become one of fashion's most recognized symbols of wealth.

339, 340 Opposite left, Dries Van Noten, Spring/Summer 1998. Van Noten's designs exemplified the modified ethnicity popular at the end of the 1990s. Opposite right, Fendi used patchwork fur to create an Op Art coat, as fashion moved towards a bolder colour statement for the new century; Autumn/Winter 2000/2001

341 The Prada 'Sport' epitomizes the role of sports shoe as fashion staple – its discreet red flash at the back is its only branding, but speaks volumes to fashion insiders; Spring/Summer 1999

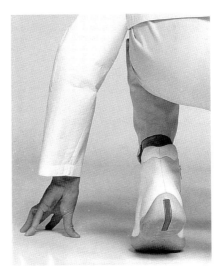

342 Handbags are eminently collectible, few more so than the Fendi baguette, perhaps the 1990s' most famous 'must-have' item. Pieces such as these are often produced on a small scale; their scarcity increases their desirability; Autumn/Winter 2000/2001

The creative currents circulating during the transitional years that mark the symbolic ending of an era and the birth of a new one are often confused. In fashion, as the millennium approached, this took the form of a backlash against the neo-bohemian trends of the mid-decade and a resurgence of tailoring for women. The balance of influence shifted towards a more severely sexy aesthetic, much of which was inspired by vintage Yves Saint Laurent from the 1970s and 1980s. Exemplified by blouses with pussycat bow collars, 'frumpy' skirt lengths and sharply tailored jackets, what had previously been a soft and layered look began to focus on high-maintenance concepts of glamour centring around an extensive use of diamanté, gold, Lurex, satin, patent leather and tweed.

Running concurrently with fashion's update on bourgeois femininity, a more literal interpretation of eighties style began to appear from younger designers catering to contemporaries who, like them, had been children in the 1980s. Focusing on early eighties 'New Wave' imagery, as popularized by singers such as Blondie and Grace Jones, key pieces included skinny masculine jackets, draped jersey dresses and customization in the guise of deliberately distressed denim, graffiti-inspired prints and post-Punk badges.

CHAPTER ELEVEN

Fashion in the twenty-first century

AT THE BEGINNING of the twenty-first century, the fashion industry has swelled to encompass increasing numbers not only of designers, brands and retailers but also of information providers able to communicate and sell fashion globally through both electronic and printed media. The pressure to conform to a single prevailing style has been lifted: while Paris, New York and Milan retain their status as the premier fashion capitals, designers operating from a multiplicity of cities, including New Delhi and Mumbai, Beijing and Hong Kong, Johannesburg and Lisbon, have developed their own distinctive identities and industries.

Since the worldwide depression took hold in 2008, designers and luxury brands have had to operate in fiercely competitive international markets. In order to secure the media coverage so critical for their image and status, huge budgets are channelled into marketing. Chanel's Autumn/Winter 2010 catwalk show, *Ill. 343* for example, was shown against a backdrop of a 265-tonne iceberg specially imported from Sweden, which took 35 ice sculptors, flown into Paris from around the world, six days to carve. In 2010 the industry mourned the tragic death by suicide of vanguard designer Alexander McQueen and in 2011 was shocked by the fall from grace of John Galliano, Dior's eclectic designer, who was sacked amid allegations of racial abuse. Both of these visionary designers were renowned for the spectacle, drama and narrative content of their catwalk shows. McQueen's Autumn/Winter 2008 show was inspired by a visit to India and *Ill. 344* a dream about a princess who lived in a six-hundred-year-old tree at the bottom of his garden. Frothy ballerina dresses were shown alongside sharp military tailoring, regal scarlet satin

343 Chanel's ready-to-wear catwalk show for Autumn/Winter 2010 featured shaggy fake-fur garments, which were shown against a giant ice sculpture.

ruched evening coats, cut-out lace and shredded knits. The models were adorned with bejewelled headpieces and slippers.

With more than a billion people watching web videos in 2011, including the latest catwalk shows, it was perhaps inevitable that film as fashion medium would be revived and rendered entirely modern by the exploitation of digital technologies. SHOWStudio, the award-winning fashion platform established by photographer Nick Knight in 2000, has been instrumental in exploring the possibilities of, and driving, this trend. Since 2003 concept-led designer Hussein Chalayan has entwined the ethos of his collections with complex themes such as the migration of peoples, using poignant abstract and narrative techniques. While Chalayan sometimes shows independently, international designers and labels – including Halston, Yves

Saint Laurent, Victor & Rolf, Alexander McQueen, Chanel, Mugler, Prada, Burberry and Gareth Pugh – have more recently shown, or incorporated, film to present their collections as part of the fashion calendar.

Among the multiplicity of fashion options presented each season, key trends can still be identified. In times of turbulent socio-economic circumstances, nostalgia becomes a dominant cultural force. By 2008 the craft-led vogue for boho-hippy trends and lean, androgynous styles was replaced with strong, structural silhouettes inspired by fashions from the 1940s and 1980s. These were characterized by shoulder pads, nipped-in waists (making belts once again desirable) and a refined palette of pale flesh tones, black and camel, or juxtapositions of bold primaries. Skinny trousers that skim the hips were replaced with high-waisted, fluid styles. Luxury fabrics that have been manipulated and embellished remain the hallmark of elite fashion and there has been a revival in the use of sequins, fur, shearling and feathers. Sensuality and gothic glamour are

344 A model from Alexander McQueen's catwalk show for Autumn/Winter 2008. The collection was inspired by a dream about an Indian princess.

evident in the resurfacing of burlesque influences, underwear as outerwear, and lingerie materials, notably in pale flesh tones and black lace.

As well as being offered multiple fashion choices, consumers can now enjoy flexible shopping opportunities 24/7. Fashion's retail landscape has been transformed by e-commerce, which is now the fastest-growing sector of the market. Between 2006 and 2011 online international fashion sales increased by 152%, significantly boosted by the new transactional websites of high street stores, while fashion applications on smartphones facilitate purchasing on the move. It is the luxury sector, which must astutely balance exclusivity with commercial imperatives, that has proved most resistant to e-commerce, fearing that luxury and online shopping are incompatible. Most designers do have a strong web presence with innovative and experiential sites, however, and will, perhaps necessarily, succumb to online trading.

Mediating between creators, retailers and consumers are online bloggers, some of whom, such as 'The Sartorialist' and 'Facehunter', have attracted a mass following; they have privileged personal – as opposed to designer-led – style and styling, not unlike ground-breaking style magazines *iD* and *The Face*, launched in the 1980s. Joining them are 'real' consumer voices who respond to trends and products via social networking sites such as Facebook and Twitter.

In order to reposition themselves as luxury fashion labels, a number of heritage brands have appointed talented designers to re-present their classics and inject the label with a new modern vigour. In Britain Burberry have enjoyed meteoric success with Christopher Bailey's creative input; Paris labels Balenciaga and Lanvin have been revived by Nicholas Ghesquière and Alber Elbaz respectively, as have Yves Saint Laurent by Stefano Pilati and Celine by Phoebe Philo. Handbags are still the 'must-have' accessory, with the most desirable models generating waiting lists of clients prepared to pay four- and five-figure sums for their luxury products. Hermès has harnessed the talents of radical Belgian designer Martin Margiela and the bad-boy of

Paris fashion, Jean-Paul Gaultier, to inject fun and modernity into its ranges, and Louis Vuitton engaged Marc Jacobs to huge critical acclaim and market success. *Ill. 345*

China is predicted to become the world's largest market for luxury goods by 2020, as fast-growing ranks of super-rich announce their style and status by indulging in elite fashion. Designers and luxury brands are not only expanding their retail operations by opening flagship stores in China, but actively addressing cultural specificities in taste. Hermès has even launched a China-specific sub-brand called Shang Xia. China is significant not only for export sales, but also for 'imported' fashion consumption in Europe: in 2011 it was 30% cheaper for the Chinese to buy luxury goods in London than at home.

While luxury goods generate the media coverage that enhances brand cachet, they do not generate the greatest profits. In order to heighten their broader public profile and boost sales of the licensed goods and diffusion lines that do create phenomenal profits, a number of designers create special ranges for the mass market. (Since these do not compete with their exclusive lines, they do not feel compromised.) Sonia Rykiel, Matthew Williamson and Comme des Garçons are among the leading international fashion names to have designed sell-out special collections for high street fashion chain H&M, while Topshop has collaborated with cutting edge British designers such as Christopher Kane and Jonathan Saunders and – perhaps most notably – supermodel and style leader Kate Moss.

345 Classic French luxury luggage brand Louis Vuitton presents a bag emblazoned with a graffiti logo design in neon pink for the fashion market. Stephen Sprouse tribute collection by Marc Jacobs for Louis Vuitton, 2009.

The extraordinary power of celebrities to shape consumer choices has been a notable feature of the 21st century. Fashion sales have rocketed when promoted by A-list actresses, top models and popular media personalities, as well as elite society. When Catherine, Duchess of Cambridge, the new wife of the second-in-line to the British throne, was shown wearing a flesh-toned bandage wrap dress by the upmarket high street retailer Reiss in May 2011, worldwide demand resulted in a same-day sell-out. With the world's media spotlight shining so intensely upon them, celebrities and the rich and titled engage stylists to shape their image and prevent faux pas. L'Wren Scott dresses Hollywood star Nicole Kidman, while pop singer sensation Lady Gaga is dressed by the Japanese-Italian stylist Nicola Formichetti, whose lack of formal fashion training did not deter Thierry Mugler from offering him the role of creative director in September 2010.

Operating online, Coolspotters (coolspotters.com) has provided a one-stop portal for identifying the styles worn by celebrities and their fictional alter egos in film and television.

346 The wedding ceremony of Prince William and Catherine Middleton in 2011. The bride wears a dress by Sarah Burton, designer at Alexander McQueen.

Sites such as ASOS (As Seen On Screen - asos.com) sell copies of clothing and accessories worn by celebrities, and those who desire a more tangible connection with their favourite celebrity can access sites that offer their 'authentic' worn clothes for hire. Turning full-circle, celebrities have capitalized on their visibility by launching their own fashion labels; perhaps the most success-ful of these has been Victoria Beckham, former pop star and wife of footballer David, whose collections of stylish dresses have been critically acclaimed and attracted a celebrity clientele.

The vogue for wearing vintage fashion – historical items of dress that reflect prevailing trends – has challenged the homo-geneity and poor quality of mass-produced fashion; it offers individual style at affordable prices and addresses environmental concerns by recycling. Kate Moss has been seminal in creating the vogue for juxtaposing vintage items with high street and top-level fashion garments. Specialist dealers operate via auction houses (the online auction site eBay is a major purveyor of vintage clothing), retail and online outlets. At the top end of the market, museum-quality items are purchased by stylists on behalf of A-list actresses such as Julia Roberts, Natalie Portman, *Ill. 347* Penélope Cruz and Angelina Jolie, who have all been photo-graphed wearing luxe-vintage for red carpet Oscar ceremonies. *Ill. 348* Major brands are tapping into this desire for individual expres-sion, including the sportswear label Nike, which offers customers a personal customization service.

While fashion is inherently ephemeral, a new term, 'fast fashion', has been coined to describe low-price, fashion-forward clothes sold on the high street. In Britain, famous for its superb high street fashion stores, it has been estimated that in 2011 the 'average' woman has around four times as many clothes as her counterpart owned in 1980. The result is that more and more energy, materials and labour resources are being expended and the landfill sites are brimming over.

What does the future hold? Although it can never replace consumption, shopping in virtual environments offers a leisure activity and outlet to express personal fashion choices that do

347, 348 Above left, supermodel and style leader Kate Moss wears a vintage dress by the French couturier Jean Dessès in 2003. Above right, Actress Sienna Miller dressed in an elegant vintage backless gown by Emanuel Ungaro for the British Academy Film Awards in 2007

not require a budget or create a carbon footprint. As we witness the rapid depletion of scarce global resources combined with the environmental consequences of over-consumption, virtual shopping might – if successfully developed – offer an alternative that is fun, carefree and sustainable.

Select Bibliography

ARNOLD, R. *Fashion, Desire and Anxiety: Image and Morality in the 20th Century.* London 2001
BOEHN, MAX VON. *Modes and Manners.* 4 vols. London 1932.
BOUCHER, P. *A History of Costume in the West.* London 1967.
BRADFIELD, N. *Historical Costumes of England.* London 1938.
— *Costume in Detail: Women's Dress 1730–1930.* London 1969.
BRADLEY, C. G. *Western World Costume.* New York 1954.
BREWARD, C. *The Hidden Consumer: Masculinites, Fashion and City Life 1860–1914.* Manchester 1999.
BROOKE, IRIS. *English Costume.* 6 vols. London 1931–5.
CHENOUNE, F. *A History of Men's Fashion.* London and New York 1946.
CUNNINGTON, C. W. *English Women's Clothing in the Nineteenth Century.* London 1937.
— *English Women's Clothing in the Present Century.* London 1952.
CUNNINGTON, C. W. and P. *Handbook of English Mediaeval Costume.* London 1952.
— *Handbook of English Costume in the Sixteenth Century.* London 1954.
— *Handbook of English Costume in the Seventeenth Century.* London 1955.
— *Handbook of English Costume in the Eighteenth Century.* London 1957.
— *Handbook of English Costume in the Nineteenth Century.* London 1959.
— *A Dictionary of English Costume.* London 1960.
DAVENPORT, N. *Book of Costume.* London 1948.
DE MARLY, D. *The History of Haute Couture, 1850–1950.* London and New York 1980.
DIOR, C. *Christian Dior and I.* New York 1957.
DRUITT, H. *A Manual of Costume as Illustrated by Monumental Brasses.* London 1906.
EICHER, J. (ed.) *Berg Encyclopedia of World Dress and Fashion.* 10 vols. Oxford and New York, 2010
EVANS, C. *Fashion at the Edge.* London and New York 2003.
— and THORNTON, M. *Women and Fashion.* London 1989.
EVANS, M. *Costume through the Ages.* London 1930.
EWING, E. *History of 20th Century Fashion.* London 1974; New York 1975.
FAIRHOLT, F. W. *Costume in England. 2 vols* London 1885.

GLYNN, P. *In Fashion: Dress in the Twentieth Century.* London 1978.
HART, A. and NORTH, S. *Fashion in Detail: From the 17th and 18th Centuries.* London 1998.
HERALD, J. *Renaissance Dress in Italy 1400–1500.* London 1982.
HOLLAND, V. *Hand-coloured Fashion Plates, 1770–1899.* London 1955.
HOWELL, G. *In Vogue.* London 1975.
JOHNSTON, L. *Nineteenth-Century Fashion in Detail.* London 2005
KEENAN, B. *Dior in Vogue.* London and New York 1981.
KELLY, F. M. and SCHWABE, R. *Historic Costume.* London, 1925.
— *A Short History of Costume and Armour.* London 1931.
LAVER, J. *Fashion and Fashion Plates.* London 1943.
— *Taste and Fashion.* London 1945.
— *Costume.* London 1963.
— *Dress.* London 1966.
LEE, S. T. (ed.) *American Fashion: the Life and Lines of Adrian, Mainbocher, McCardell, Norell, Trigère.* New York 1975; London 1976.
LESTER, K. M. *Historic Costume.* London 1942.
LURIE, A. *The Language of Clothes.* London and New York 1982.
MENDES, V. and DE LA HAYE, A. *20th Century Fashion.* London and New York 1999.
MILBANK, C. R. *Couture: The Great Fashion Designers.* London 1985.
MULVAGH, J. *Vogue: History of 20th Century Fashion.* London 1988.
O'HARA, G. *The Encyclopaedia of Fashion.* London and New York 1986.
PEACOCK, J. *20th Century Fashion: The Complete Sourcebook.* London and New York 1993.
— *Men's Fashion: The Complete Sourcebook.* London and New York 1996.
— *Fashion Accessories: The Complete 20th Century Sourcebook.* London and New York 2000.
PLANCHÉ, V. R. *A Cyclopaedia of Costume.* 2 vols. London 1876, 1879.
POLHEMUS, T. *Streetstyle.* London and New York 1994.
SCOTT, M. *Late Gothic Europe 1400–1500.* London 1981.
TAYLOR, L. *The Study of Dress History.* Manchester 2002.
— *Establishing Dress History.* Manchester 2004.
VAN THIENEN, F. *The Great Age of Holland* ('Costume of the Western World'). London 1951.
WILCOX, C. AND MENDES, V. *Modern Fashion in Detail.* London 1991.

List of Illustrations

300

Painter. Greek, early fifth century BC. London, British Museum.

30 Female dancer. Etruscan, end sixth century BC. Bronze. Boston, Museum of Fine Arts.

31 Dancers from Tomb of Leopards, Tarquinia. Etruscan, first quarter of fifth century BC. Wall-painting.

32 Vestal virgin. Roman, second century AD. Marble statue. Rome, National Museum. *Photo Mansell Collection.*

33 The Emperor Tiberius. Roman, first century AD. Marble statue. Paris, Louvre. *Photo Giraudon.*

34 'Bikini girl' from Imperial Villa, Piazza Armerina, Sicily. Roman, late third century AD. Mosaic. *Photo André Held.*

35 Drawing of Roman statues from *Monuments de Sculptures Antiques et Modernes*, Vauther and Lacour, Paris 1839.

36 Head of unknown Roman lady from pagan grave beneath St Peter's, Rome. By courtesy of Reverenda Fabrica della Basilica di San Pietro.

37 Head from group of Three Graces. Roman. Siena, Museo dell'Opera della Cattedrale. *Photo Alinari.*

38 Head of Roman girl. Hellenistic sculpture in Egyptian style, date unknown. Rome, Capitoline Museum. *Photo Georgina Masson.*

39 Head of unknown woman. Roman, Flavian period, second century AD. Marble. Rome, Capitoline Museum.

40 Sarcophagus. Roman, late fourth century AD. Marble. Milan, S. Ambrogio Cathedral. *Photo Mansell Collection.*

41 Procession of female saints. Byzantine, set up *c.* 561. Mosaic. Ravenna, Church of St Apollinare Nuovo. *Photo Alinari.*

42 The Empress Theodora and her suite. Byzantine, 500–26. Mosaic. Ravenna, San Vitale. *Photo Alinari.*

43 Head of the Emperor Justinian. Byzantine, 500–26. Mosaic. Ravenna, San Vitale.

44 Head of the Empress Theodora. Byzantine, 500–26. Mosaic. Ravenna, San Vitale.

45 Four parts of Empire – Sclavinia, Germania, Gallia and Roma – paying homage to Otto III enthroned. Ottonian, 997–1000. Gospel book of Otto III. Munich, Staatsbibliothek. *Photo Hirmer Verlag.*

46 King Edward the Confessor from the Bayeux tapestry. Late eleventh century. Bayeaux, Musée de la Tapisserie. *Photo Giraudon.*

47 Preparations for a wedding from *The Woman of Andros*, Terence. MS executed at St Albans, mid twelfth century Illustrations goes back through a Carolingian copy to a late classical manuscript. Oxford, Bodleian Library, MS Auct. F.2.13, f. 4v.

48 Crusader doing homage, from an English psalter. Thirteenth century. London, British Museum, MS Royal 2AXXII, f. 220.

49 Shepherds, *c.* 1150, from tympanum of 'Portal of the Virgin', west porch, Chartres Cathedral. *Photo Martin Hürlimann.*

50 Sainted king and queen, *c.* 1150, west porch, Chartres Cathedral. *Photo Bildarchiv Marburg.*

51 The Lady Uta, founderfigure, *c.* 1245, west choir, Naumburg Cathedral. *Photo Helga Schmidt-Glassner.*

52 Peasant costume from the Luttrell Psalter. English, *c.* 1335–40. London, British Museum, MS 42130, f. 170.

53 Sir Georffrey Luttrell with his wife and daughter-in-law, from the Luttrell Psalter. English, *c.* 1335–40. London, British Museum, MS 42130, f. 202v.

54 Dame Margarete de Cobham, from Cobham, Kent. English, 1375. Monumental brass rubbing. London, Victoria and Albert Museum.

55 John Coop, from Stoke Fleming, Devon. English, 1391. Monumental brass rubbing. London, by courtesy of the Society of Antiquaries. *Photo C. Bibbey.*

56 Agnes Salmon, from Arundel, Sussex. English, 1430. Monumental brass rubbing. London, Victoria and Albert Museum.

57 Robert Skern, from Kingston-upon-Thames, Surrey. English, 1437. Monumental brass rubbing. London, Victoria and Albert Museum.

58 Probably Elizabeth Hasylden, from Little Chesterford, Essex. English, *c.* 1480. Monumental brass rubbing.

59 William Midwinter (d. 1501), from Northleach, Gloucestershire. English, early sixteenth century. Monumental brass rubbing.

60 *The Marriage of Giovanni (?) Arnolfini and Giovanna Cenami (?)*, 1434, Jan van Eyck. London, by courtesy of the Trustees of the National Gallery. *Photo National Gallery.*

61 Male and female costume, *c.* 1470. Engraving by Israel van Meckenem.

62 Male and female costume, *c.* 1485. Engraving by Israel van Meckenem.

63 *Wedding of Boccaccio Adimari, c.* 1470, Florentine school. Florence, Accademia. *Photo Scala.*

64 *Duchess of Urbino*, after 1473, Piero della Francesca. Florence, Uffizi.

301

65 *Portrait of a lady in red*, c. 1470, Florentine school. London, by courtesy of the Trustees of the National Gallery.

66 *Margaret of Denmark, Queen of Scotland* (detail), 1476, ascribed to Hugo van der Goes. Edinburgh, Holyrood Palace. Reproduced by gracious permission of Her Majesty the Queen.

67 Philip the Good, Duke of Burgundy, receiving a copy of the *Chroniques de Hainaut*. Flemish, 1448. Miniature. Brussels, Bibliothèque Royale de Belgique, MS 9242, f. 1r.

68 Christine de Pisan presenting her book of poems to Isabel of Bavaria, Queen of France. French, early fifteenth century. Miniature from *Works* of Christine de Pisan. London, British Museum, MS Harley 4431, f. 3r.

69 Detail from *Chronique d'Angleterre*, Jean de Wavrin. Flemish, fifteenth century. London, British Museum, MS Royal 14.E.IV.

70 *Portrait of a lady*, c. 1455, Rogier van der Weyden. Washington, National Gallery of Art, Andrew Mellon Collection.

71 *Giovanna Tornabuoni*, 1488, Domenico Ghirlandaio. Lugano, Thyssen Collection. *Photo Brunel Lugano.*

72 *Nuremberg housewife and Venetian lady*, 1495, Albrecht Dürer. Drawing. Frankfurt, Städelsches Kunstinstitut.

73 Jacob Fugger 'the Rich', the Emperor's banker with his chief accountant Matthäus Schwarz, 1519. Miniature. Brunswick, Herzog Anton Ulrich-Museum.

74 German *Landsknecht*, c. 1530. Design for stained-glass window. London, Victoria and Albert Museum.

75 The Swiss Guards, detail from *Mass of Bolsena*, 1511–14, Raphael. Fresco. Rome, Vatican, Stanza dell' Eliodoro.

76 *Duke Henry of Saxony and his wife*, 1514, Lucas Cranach. Dresden, Gemäldegalerie.

77 *Katherine, Duchess of Saxony*, 1514, Lucas Cranach. Dresden, Gemäldegalerie.

78 *Katherina Knoblauchin*, 1532, Conrad Faber. Dublin, National Gallery of Ireland.

79 *Portrait of an unknown man*, before 1540, Bartolommeo Veneto. Rome, Galleria Nazionale. *Photo Mansell Collection.*

80 *Francis I of France*, first half of sixteenth century, attributed to François Clouet. Paris, Louvre. *Photo Garanger-Giraudon.*

81 *Helen of Bavaria*, c. 1563–6, Hans Schöpfer. Munich, Bayerische Staatsgemäldesammlungen.

82 *Jane Seymour*, c. 1536–7, Hans Holbein. Vienna, Kunsthistorisches Museum.

83 *Henry VIII*, based on original of 1537, school of Holbein. Liverpool, Walker Art Gallery.

84 Costume plate, c. 1560. Engraving by Jost Amman. London, British Museum.

85 *The Ambassadors*, 1533, Hans Holbein. London, by courtesy of the Trustees of the National Gallery.

86 *Thomas Cranmer*, 1546, Gerhardt Flicke. London, National Portrait Gallery.

87 *Emperor Charles V with his dog*, 1532, Titian. Madrid, Prado. *Photo Mas.*

88 *Anne of Austria, Queen of Spain*, 1571, Sanchez Coello. Vienna, Kunsthistorisches Museum.

89 *A tailor*, probably c. 1571, Giovanni Battista Moroni. London, by courtesy of the Trustees of the National Gallery.

90 *Portrait of a young man*, probably c. 1540, Angelo Bronzino. New York, The Metropolitan Museum of Art, H. O. Havemeyer Collection.

91 *Pierre Quthe*, 1562, François Clouet. Paris, Louvre. *Photo Giraudon.*

92 *Mary I, Queen of England*, 1554, Antonis Mor. Madrid, Prado. *Photo Mansell Collection.*

93 *Elizabeth I, 'Rainbow Portrait'*, c. 1600, style of Marcus Gheeraerts. Reproduced by permission of the Marquess of Salisbury KG, Hatfield House. *Photo Courtauld Institute of Art.*

94 *Magdalena, Duchess of Neuburg*, c. 1613, formerly attributed to Peter Candid (de Witte). Munich, Alte Pinakothek. *Photo Joachim Blauel.*

95 *Queen Elizabeth at Blackfriars*, c. 1600, Marcus Gheeraerts. Collection Simon Wingfield Digby MP, Sherborne Castle. *Photo Fleming.*

96 Elizabeth, Briget and Susan, 1589, from tomb of their grandmother Mildred, Lady Burghley. London, Westminster Abbey. Crown copyright. *Photo Royal Commission on Historical Monuments.*

97 Sir Robert Burghley, 1589, from tomb of his mother Mildred, Lady Burghley. London, Westminster Abbey. Crown copyright. *Photo Royal Commission on Historical Monuments.*

98 Elizabeth costume, from *Description of England.* Anonymous drawing. Flemish, late sixteenth century. London, British Museum, MS Add. 28330.

99 *Rubens and his wife Isabella Brant*, 1610, Peter Paul Rubens. Munich, Alte Pinakothek.

100 *Sigmund Feierabendt, the bibliophile*, 1587. Engraving by J. Sadeler.

303

after Moreau le Jeune.

156 *Les Adieux, c.* 1777. Engraving after Moreau le Jeune.

157 *Le Rendez-vous pour Marly, c.* 1776. Engraving after Moreau le Jeune.

158 *The Promenade at Carlisle House,* 1781. Mezzotint by J.R. Smith.

159 *Coiffure sans redoute, c.* 1785. Engraving.

160 *Robe à la Polonaise,* 1778. Fashion plate from *Galerie des Modes.*

161 Dressmaker carrying a pair of paniers, *c.* 1778. Fashion plate from *Galerie des Modes.*

162 Walking dresses, 1795. Fashion plate from Heideloff's *Gallery of Fashion.*

163 Summer dresses, 1795. Fashion plate from Heideloff's *Gallery of Fashion.*

164 Day dresses, 1796. Fashion plate from Heideloff's *Gallery of Fashion.*

165 *Point de Convention, c.* 1801, Louis-Léopold Boilly. French private collection. *Photo Federico Arborio Mella.*

166 Morning dress, February 1799. Fashion plate.

167 Ball dress, 1800. Fashion plate from *Journal des Luxus und der Moden, Weimar.*

168 *Madame Récamier,* 1802, François Gérard. Paris, Musée Carnavalet. *Photo Giraudon.*

169 *I have not learned my book, Mamma, c.* 1800. Stipple engraving by Adam Buck.

170 *La belle Zélie,* 1806, J.-A.-D. Ingres. Rouen, Musée des Beaux-Arts. *Photo Giraudon.*

171 English outdoor dress, *c.* 1807–10. Manchester, Museum of Costume, Platt Hall.

172 Male and female walking dress, 1810. Fashion plate from *Journal des Dames et des Modes.*

173 Summer walking dresses, 1817. Fashion plate from *Journal des Dames et des Modes.*

174 *Thomas Bewick, c.* 1810. Engraving by F. Bacon after James Ramsay.

175 *Captain Barclay, 'the celebrated pedestrian', c.* 1820. Engraving.

176 Male and female walking dress, 1818. Fashion plate.

177 Kensington Garden dresses for June 1808. Fashion plate from *Le Beau Monde.*

178 *Monstrosities of 1822.* Etching by George Cruikshank.

179 Walking dress, 1819. Fashion plate.

180 Carriage dress, 1824. Fashion plate from *The Lady's Magazine.*

181 French and German costumes, 1826. Fashion plate from *Journal des Dames et des Modes.*

182 Evening and morning dress, 1831. Fashion plate from *La Belle Assemblée,* London.

183 Male and female riding costume, 1831. Fashion plate.

184 Dresses, 1829. Fashion plate.

185 Pelisse robe, silk brocade, English, 1831–3. London, Victoria and Albert Museum.

186 Gentlemen's morning dress, 1834. Fashion plate.

187 *In the garden,* 1840. Fashion plate from *Allgemeine Modenzeitung,* Leipzig.

188 *Florence Nightingale and her sister Parthenope, c.* 1836, W. White. London, National Portrait Gallery.

189 Male costume, 1849. Fashion plate.

190 *Convalescence, c.* 1845. Engraving by Charles Rolls after Eugène Lami.

191 Day dresses, *c.* 1848. Fashion plate from *Le Follet.*

192 Winter dress, 1847. Fashion plate from *Le Follet.*

Mantles for the theatre, 1835. Fashion plate from *Allgemeine Modenzeitung,* Leipzig.

193 Day dresses, 1853. Fashion plate from *Le Follet.*

194 *A Windy Corner,* 1864. Anonymous lithograph. London, Victoria and Albert Museum.

195 Girls in crinoline dresses and pantaloons, 1853. From *Die Tafel Birnen.*

196 Crinoline petticoat, *c.* 1860. Fashion plate.

197 Paris fashions for September 1859. Fashion plate from *Illustrated London News.*

198 *In a box at the Opera,* 1857. Fashion plate from *Le Follet.*

199 Mrs Amelia Bloomer, *c.* 1850. Anonymous engraving.

200 *Une tournure à faire tourner toutes les têtes!,* 1858. Lithograph by Charles Vernier. London, Victoria and Albert Museum.

201 *The Empress Eugénie and her maids of honour, c.* 1860, Francis Xavier Winterhalter. Compiègne Chateau. *Photo Giraudon.*

202 Crinoline dress, *c.* 1860, by Worth. Drawing on lithograph model. London, Victoria and Albert Museum.

203 London and Paris fashions for June 1864. Fashion plate.

204 *Women in the garden,* 1866–7, Claude Monet. Paris, Louvre. *Photo Giraudon.*

205 London and Paris fashions for March 1869. Fashion plate.

206 Headdresses, August 1870. Fashion plate from *Le Journal des Modes.*

207 Duke of Edinburgh and Grand Duchess Marie Alexandrovna, *c.* 1870. Fashion plate from *Tailor and Cutter.*

208 Lady's and child's dresses, September 1873. Fashion plate from *Journal des Desmoiselles.*

209 *Madame Moitessier,* 1844/5–56. J.-A.-D. Ingres. London, by courtesy of the Trustees of the National Gallery. *Photo National Gallery.*

311 Jersey dress by Jean Muir, 1973. *Photo Vogue magazine,* © *Condé Nast.*

312 Punks on King's Road, London, 1980. *Photo Sue Snell.*

313 Design by Vivienne Westwood, from the 'Buffalo' collection, Autumn/Winter 1982/83. *Photo Niall McInerney.*

314 Wrap, shirt and dirndl skirt by Issey Miyake, London, 1982. *Photo courtesy of Issey Miyake.*

315 Design by Norma Kamali, from the 'Sweats' collection, Spring/Summer 1981. *Photo courtesy of Norma Kamali.*

316 Design by Azzedine Alaïa, Spring/Summer 1986. *Photo Niall McInerney.*

317 Suit by Thierry Mugler, Autumn/Winter 1989/90. *Photo courtesy of Thierry Mugler.*

318 Design by Karl Lagerfeld for Chanel, Spring/Summer 1993. *Photo Niall McInerney.*

319 From a Moschino Couture advertising campaign, Autumn/Winter 1988/89. Model: Violetta Sanchez. *Photo Moschino.*

320 Raw silk jacket, linen culottes, by Ralph Lauren, 1982. *Photo Albert Watson,* Vogue *magazine,* © *Condé Nast.*

321 Designs by Calvin Klein, Autumn/Winter 1983/84. *Photo courtesy of Calvin Klein.*

322 Design by Rei Kawakubo/ Comme des Garçons, Autumn/Winter 1983/84. *Photo Niall McInerney.*

323 Tailored suit by Giorgio Armani, Spring/Summer 1989. *Photo Niall McInerney.*

324 Design by Missoni, Autumn/Winter 1987/88. *Photo courtesy of Missoni.*

325 Design by Yohji Yamamoto, Spring/Summer 1989. *Photo courtesy of Yohji Yamamoto.*

326 Tailored suit by Paul Smith,

Spring/Summer 1994. *Photo Niall McInerney.*

327 Drawing by Christian Lacroix, for his Autumn/Winter 1994/95 collection. *Drawing courtesy of Christian Lacroix.*

328 Design by Christian Lacroix, Summer 1987. *Photo Jean-François Gaté.*

329 Menswear design by Jean-Paul Gaultier, Spring/Summer 1994. *Photo Niall McInerney.*

330 Design by Anna Sui, Spring/ Summer 1994. *Photo Niall McInerney.*

331 Design by Gucci, Spring/ Summer 1999. *Photo courtesy of Gucci.*

332 Design by Gucci, Spring/ Summer 1999. *Photo courtesy of Gucci.*

333 Design by John Galliano for Dior Couture, Spring/ Summer 1997. *Photo Sean Ellis.*

334 Design by Alexander McQueen, Spring/Summer 2001. *Photo Chris Moore. Courtesy of Alexander McQueen.*

335 Design by Helmut Lang, Autumn/Winter 1998. *Photo Chris Moore.*

336 Suit and suit carrier by Ozwald Boateng, Spring/ Summer 2001. *Photo Giannoni G. Courtesy of Ozwald Boateng.*

337 Design by Prada, Spring/ Summer 1996. *Photo courtesy of Prada.*

338 Design by Prada, Spring/ Summer 1997. *Photo courtesy of Prada.*

339 Design by Dries Van Noten, Spring/Summer 1998. *Photo courtesy of Dries Van Noten.*

340 Design by Fendi, Womenswear Collection, Autumn/ Winter 2000/2001. *Photo courtesy of Fendi.*

341 'Prada Sport' shoe, Spring/ Summer 1999. *Photo courtesy of Prada.*

342 Handbag design by Fendi, Autumn/Winter 2000/2001. *Photo courtesy of Fendi.*

343 Chanel Autumn/Winter 2010. *Photo Maria Valentino for the* Washington Post/Getty Images.

344 Alexander McQueen Autumn/Winter 2008. *Photo Rex Features.*

345 Louis Vuitton bag from 2009 tribute collection to Stephen Sprouse by Marc Jacobs. © *Louis Vuitton.*

346 Prince William, Duke of Cambridge and Catherine, Duchess of Cambridge. *Photo Suzanne Plunkett – WPA Pool/ Getty Images.*

347 Kate Moss wearing vintage dress. *Photo Matt Baron/BEI/ Rex Features.*

348 Sienna Miller wearing vintage dress. *Photo Stuart Atkins/Rex Features.*

Index